P9-EDT-694

TRADITIONAL HOUSES OF

RURAL ITALY

TRADITIONAL HOUSES OF
RURAL ITALY

PAUL DUNCAN

PHOTOGRAPHY BY
JOHN FERRO SIMS

Abbeville Press • Publishers
New York • London • Paris

JACKET ILLUSTRATIONS:
FRONT: *A* casa colonica *(farmhouse)*
in Tuscany.
BACK: *Gothic and classical styles combine*
in the windows and door of this Venetian
town House (left)*; a Tuscan doorway*
dating from the fifteenth century (right).

Copyright © Collins & Brown 1993
Text copyright © Paul Duncan 1993
Photographs copyright © John Ferro Sims 1993
First American Edition

Published by Abbeville Press. All rights reserved under international copyright
conventions. No part of this book may be reproduced or utilized in any form or
by any means, electronic or mechanical, including photocopying, recording, or by
any information storage and retrieval system, without permission in writing from
the publisher. Inquiries should be addressed to Abbeville Publishing Group,
488 Madison Avenue, New York, New York 10022. Printed and bound in Italy.

A CIP catalog record for this book is available from the British Library

Editor : Sarah Hoggett
Art Director : Roger Bristow
Designers : Ruth Hope, Gail Jones and Rowan Seymour

FRONTISPIECE: MASTER OF ALL IT
SURVEYS
Each casa colonica *(farmhouse)*
jealously guards its own patch of
Tuscany. For as far as the eye can see,
the brows of the gentle Tuscan hills
around Siena are crowned with
farmhouses in varying states of repair.

CONTENTS

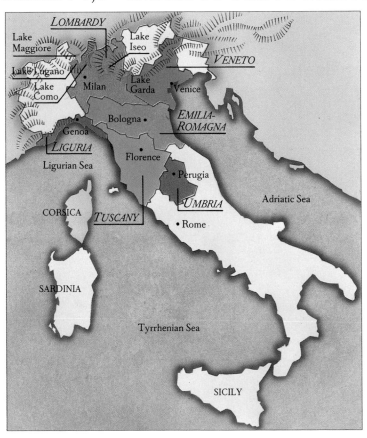

INTRODUCTION

M ANY PEOPLE'S VISION OF rural Italy is based on what flashes past the windows of their car as they rush along the *autostrada* between cities. In most cases a magical vision, it is none the less an incomplete one because just a few minutes away, beyond the hard shoulder and the motorway junctions, lies another Italy, an Italy of remote hill towns, farmhouses and wayside shrines.

Away from the great palaces, the houses and the magnificent churches of urban Florence, Pisa, Venice and Bologna, buildings are judged by quite different criteria. If a 300-year-old rural building has stood the test of time and still works satisfactorily for its modern occupants, then it too can be called 'great'. Farm buildings are often the culmination of centuries of trial and error: if a building's modern users are happy with it, then its original builders got it right.

In addition to being admirably suited to their function, Italian rural buildings invariably show some sign that their builder was aware of the predominant architectural style of his region. Buildings in the orbit of Florence, for example, whether they date from the fifteenth or the nineteenth century, are strongly influenced by the Renaissance in their proportions, detailing and basic style. There are, of course, exceptions, as this book will show.

The look of Italy's rural buildings varies from one region to another, depending on what materials are available locally. In Emilia-Romagna, for example, buildings are mostly of brick, while in Tuscany a tawny stone sometimes dressed with marble is used. In Liguria the roof coverings are grey granite slates, while Umbrian builders prefer either slate or terracotta pantiles. Then, as now, builders used what was to hand, particularly in regions that were inaccessible. Thus a lot of marble is used in the provinces around Pisa and the quarries at nearby Carrara and far less of it across the Apennines in the Emilia-Romagna — not all that far away. Similarly, on the edges of the Venetian lagoons, reeds are turned into thatch for the walls and roofs. These natural variations have been reinforced by

LEFT: ORTA SAN GIULIO, PIEDMONT
An undistinguished group of buildings is redeemed by the presence of a fading fresco of the risen Christ. Granite roof tiles and plaster rendering give no hint as to what materials lie beneath — in this case, stone.

historical differences: what was favoured in one area was not necessarily possible in another because of, say, war which tends to stifle cultural interchange and trade.

Although there may have been a common pool of ideas and ideals in a particular period (take, for example, the Renaissance which is one of the richest periods in Italian architecture), it was usually local traditions and styles that dictated the overall appearance of a rural building. This might explain why a Tuscan farmhouse is so dramatically different from one in the Veneto, even though they have common points of use. It also explains why, if you dig a little deeper, you will find that a rural dwelling in the orbit of, say, Ferrara is not necessarily the same as one near Bologna, just 47 kilometres (30 miles) away, even though both are in Emilia-Romagna. Likewise the Pisan style is not quite like the Florentine, even though they are separated by just 89 kilometres (55 miles). All this adds to the variety of not just farmhouses and cottages but barns, stables, pigsties, sheds, chapels, wayside shrines and above all the remote villages and hamlets locked into a countryside the colour of dust.

Thus far, this might be a statement of the obvious. But buildings are also a key to a region's way of life. In the absence of written records chronicling the day-to-day lives of a rural population, buildings are often the only tangible remains of those who built them — all the more so in districts where poverty, a fact of life handed down from generation to generation, meant that money was hardly ever available to alter the buildings substantially. Running repairs, and perhaps adding to an existing property, were all that most people ever aspired to; and they were only too happy to occupy houses built by their ancestors. They worked well; and the basic needs of people whose lives were governed by seasonal cycles changed little if at all. Quite simply, what was good for one generation was almost certainly good for another two centuries later. Provided you know how to read these buildings — and examples over 500 years old are not difficult to find — it is possible to unlock a number of secrets about their occupants that would otherwise be missed.

Tuscany and parts of Umbria apart, a great many of Italy's rural buildings are still used today in a way that approximates to their

ABOVE: BROKEN BUT NOT BEATEN
Even after years of neglect, this embattled façade heroically resists erosion. All it needs is a superficial overhaul.

ABOVE: BELVIO, NEAR COMO, LOMBARDY
This cheeky — and very unusual — trompe l'oeil wall decoration is the poor man's answer to the question of what to do with an otherwise plain façade. To attract attention to it, why not paint it as if it was wallpaper?

original builders' intentions. What is so agreeable about them is their scale, which is generally human and manageable. Built by working people for their own use, using unadulterated, natural materials, this strikes a chord deep within us. Unlike the landowners, whose entrances were filled with oblique references to social standing and wealth, the builders of these dwellings had nothing to prove. There might be some clue as to the stylistic period in which they were built — the cut of the stone lintel and the doorposts, for example — but superfluous ornament and decoration are generally held at bay. If they exist at all, they are more often incidental than deliberately planned for: a relieving arch above a window or a door might provide a patterned feature in a flat wall of otherwise horizontal blocks; bands of terracotta bricks might alternate with others of coarse, tawny stone or shiny, black slate as a result of patching and rebuilding over the years; a row of bricks might be up-ended or placed at an angle so that it protrudes from the wall, providing a pillow at eaves level for roof trusses; apertures in the wall of a pigeon loft might be triangular or round depending on the builder's whim or the materials he had to hand.

LEFT: MENAGGIO IN NORTHERN ITALY· *This house relies on very high-quality painted and incised decoration instead of architectural adornments.*

ABOVE: VERBANIA, PIEDMONT
Carved wooden gargoyles add an exotic note to the façade of this villa which is already enriched by its saffron colour and eighteenth-century window surround. The latter is adorned with scrolls à rocaille – shell-like, coral-like forms, c-curves and s-curves.

LEFT: IN THE FERRARESE,
EMILIA-ROMAGNA
The one remaining wall exhibits three characteristics of the typical Emilian barn: extensive brickwork, decorative panels of pierced brickwork to aerate the stored crop, and simple, dignified architecture.

One of the most intriguing things about traditional rural buildings, wherever they may be, is that they tend to be at one with their landscape. The relationship between the two is a happy one: it is as if the builders have acknowledged a subordinate role for their structures, in some subconscious way paying homage to the power of Nature. These buildings appear always to have been there, weathering silently, boiling under the same sun, being battered by the same gales and washed by the same rainfall as their surroundings.

Stumbling across a derelict farmhouse or an abandoned village is an exciting experience. Unless the terrain has been ravaged by an earthquake, or the structures have been exceptionally shoddily built, these rural buildings, continuously well maintained, are hard to erase. They stand the test of time and despite, say, a caved-in roof or the absence of window panes, it is not difficult to imagine the lives led in the stone-flagged kitchens or the silent cobbled alleyways.

But why the abandonment? Where are the wood piles, and the hay, and where are the cattle that lived in the undercrofts of the buildings? Where are the demi-johns of home made wine and the jars of tomato preserves that once filled the cellars? Why aren't the ovens warm and the olive presses in the barns squeezing out oil?

All over Italy, particularly in the 1950s and 1960s, upheavals and land reforms emptied out parts of the countryside. Until the mid-1950s most Italians still earned their living in the traditional sectors of the economy such as small, technologically backward, labour-intensive farms. Life here was hard. At the end of the 1940s agrarian reforms had sought to increase the amount of smallholding property, but this did not lead to a golden age of peasant farming. Instead, many people simply gave up the battle and left the land altogether. Nowadays many country people are only part-time farmers and they have Roman and Milanese weekenders as neighbours. Attracted by the simplicity of rural life, this new breed of country dwellers has come in search of an antidote to a frenetic urban existence. The coarse rusticity of country buildings has something elemental about it. Such buildings provide a buffer zone between a totally committed 'back to nature' existence and a sophisticated urban one; herein lies the single most appealing aspect of the rural buildings of Italy.

ABOVE: AMELIA, UMBRIA
Years of neglect have rendered this village church a wreck, its method of construction exposed and weather-beaten, the stucco roundel bashed and clinging on only by some act of God. Only the beautifully cut stones of the arch have survived intact, as solid and as crisp as the day they were put there.

TUSCANY

THE TUSCANS ARE AMONGST the most envied people living in Italy today. They inhabit a land which is most people's idea of Eden. Shelley, who took refuge there in 1818, called it a paradise; while Dr Johnson before him was conscious of a certain inferiority that went with never having been there.

Tuscany is a garden in the spring; in the summer this paradise changes to an inferno, the raging heat exaggerated by the deep, hot, earth colours of the landscape. Farmsteads, barns, chapels, towns and villages echo the colours and textures of these surroundings, becoming almost one with them. This is a charmed, civilized landscape of cypresses and umbrella pines, terraces of vines and olives; and a Tuscan farmhouse, especially one within spitting distance of a chapel containing a Renaissance fresco, is a much coveted prize. If the farmhouse itself dates from the fifteenth century, even better: as a relic of the Renaissance, it is a tangible reminder of a period in which Tuscany, and Florence in particular, led the way to a new world of Art, Architecture, Sciences, Literature and Humanities. Fostered by the wealth of the ruling Medici family, this era of enlightenment eclipsed the fog of the Middle Ages.

Tuscany is officially divided into nine provinces, each centred on one of the region's bigger cities such as Florence or Pisa, Lucca or Arezzo. However, and rather confusingly for outsiders, the Tuscans give their territory other colloquial names: the Casentino, the Garfagnana, the Mugello, Chianti, the Valdichiana, the Versilia and the Maremma are just seven of these. For Tuscans these very names are enough to evoke an image of all that is best about Tuscany: the climate, the food and wine, the character of the native population, the beauty of the landscape.

Two of the most lovely of these regions are the Casentino and the Chianti. The Casentino takes in the hilly upper reaches of the Arno (the river that runs through Florence and Pisa), a remote area squeezed in between Umbria and the Marche, and the Pratomagno Hills to the

LEFT: WATCHTOWER TURNED DWELLING
Guarding a village on a hillside overlooking the valley, this stone-built lookout tower turns its little square windows defiantly towards what was once a hostile landscape.

south-east of Florence. Chianti occupies the huge sweep of land between Florence and Siena.

In the Casentino practically everything but the valley bottoms is swathed in magnificent thick forests of beech, chestnut and fir. No main routes through Tuscany pass by the Casentino so it is a rare, unspoiled backwater. In fact, it can have altered little since the thirteenth century, when the great Florentine poet Dante was imprisoned by the ferocious Counts Guidi in their castle at Porciano not far from Poppi.

Dotted about the Casentino, in the Arno basin and in the little side valleys leading away into the hills, are small hill villages and towns. Some of the former consist of nothing more than a handful of houses randomly scattered across a slope, and a church. Some are walled, the houses huddled beneath the remnants of a tower or the core of a castle. The village where Michelangelo was born, Caprese Michelangelo (south-east of Bibbiena), is one such place. It was once a small fortress, built of bleached beige stone, into which the people who worked in the fields down below could retreat with their cattle when the warring Middle Ages – in which the Casentino played a less than gentle role – became more than they could bear.

Porciano, further up the valley, is another such village (still lived in, however), and the ruins of the Castello di Romena another. At Porciano the villagers lived in little cottages, at most two storeys high, which tightly encircle the walls of the fortress in concentric rings. Narrow alleys between the rings lead to the fortress of which only a single, immensely thick, rough-stone tower now remains.

Towns like Poppi and Bibbiena occupy rocky eminences from which the southern approach to the Casentino from their aggressive neighbour, Arezzo, could be watched. Poppi grew up in the shadow of one of Tuscany's most magnificent castles, built in the mould of Florence's Palazzo Vecchio. From the Middle Ages to the Renaissance the local population found it safer and less disruptive to live up here, within the protective town walls, than in the valley below. Consequently the houses lining its streets are no ordinary dwellings; they combine the characteristics of urban house and rural homestead and in the past the town would have assumed the functions of a giant

RIGHT: HILL TOWN EYRIE
The hill town, with the rough texture of its walls and roofs, seems indivisible from its surroundings.

farmyard. Those who worked the land would simply have left Poppi each morning to take their cattle to pasture, returning with their animals in the evening.

Poppi's main artery is flanked on either side by a vaulted arcade gouged from the ground floors of the low heavy houses lining the street. Apart from the patterns in the worn brick pavements, the only other decoration is carved stone capitals on the piers of the arcades. Otherwise Poppi's houses have a solid and workaday character: the population was concerned with staying alive rather than with superfluous matters like the external appearance of their dwellings.

Beneath some of the houses are storerooms and barns, still used in very many cases to keep the firewood, perhaps even a tractor and almost certainly a Fiat. At one time cattle lived behind their great wooden double doors; and at dawn the old stone-flagged streets of Poppi would have echoed with the clopping of their hooves as they were herded down into the fields for the day. Some of these undercrofts are entered from the main street; others open from the alleys sloping off down the hill between blocks of houses. (These

RIGHT: TIME STANDS STILL
Various architectural detailings have been incorporated piecemeal onto this house. From an Ionic capital springs the whitewashed arch of an arcade; beyond, the simple geometry of an upper window is characteristic of the fourteenth century.

RIGHT: THE *CASA COLONICA*
Many rural buildings, like this still-inhabited farmhouse, are untouched by time. Outward signs of the twentieth century are hard to find.

RIGHT: FAÇADE ADORNMENTS
The stemme, *or coats of arms, of long defunct families have been stuck to the wall of the local town hall. Whether cut from granite or marble, or fashioned from glazed terracotta, each one is a becoming addition to the ancient façade.*

RIGHT: PANTILES, OLD AND NEW
The formal linear pattern of this roof mimics the rows of vines on the Chianti hillside below. Pantiles, the colour of the local clay, are hard-wearing. Use and re-use gives them their mottled patina.

blocks are known as *isole*, islands.) Nowadays Poppi is a quiet backwater. Although wine, olive oil and the odd chicken might be kept in the undercroft, most people work in Arezzo. The older inhabitants of the town still trundle out into the fields to get firewood, but that is more from force of habit than necessity.

More sophisticated than Poppi is the Valdichiana town of Pienza which has all the attributes of a large centre – castle, cathedral, palaces. It is also filled with more ordinary houses, a great many of which date from the fifteenth century. These houses are typical of agricultural centres the length and breadth of Tuscany where the population was mostly a 'bedroom' community of farmers and labourers who spent their days working outside the town walls in the wheatfields, olive groves, orchards and vineyards, and their nights within.

Large areas of Pienza were rebuilt in the fifteenth century after one of its inhabitants became Pope Pius II. He was a great Renaissance figure, responsible for transforming Pienza into a city of art with a cathedral, papal palace and central piazza. At his command, whole neighbourhoods were demolished and new houses re-erected on the

via
borgo

LEFT: IN NEED OF A FACELIFT

An old house straddling the gateway into a village has been fashioned from the ancient protective village walls. Large stones, once covered with stucco, are gradually weathering at their edges.

stumps of the old, the 'before' and 'after' periods of building work still evident today. To our eyes, the façades look quite messy and irregular – unfinished even. But at one time each house must once have been plastered over so that what lay beneath was hidden.

Other houses, instead of being demolished, were simply enlarged, with extra storeys added on top. The join between the two parts is evident in the differing style of the pointing and the size and colour of the bricks. Façades were given a face-lift by the addition of cornices: cornice strips of carved stone, running the length of a block of houses, mark each storey of the building; while the street corners are emphasized by the addition of sandstone quoins – dressed stones at the corner of buildings, a common sight all over Tuscany.

The design and layout of such houses has a long history in Italy and can be traced back through the Middle Ages and into Antiquity. They are known as *casette a schiera* which, roughly translated, means a terrace of small, upright, workers' houses. On the ground floor is a workshop with a wide door on to the street. Beside this, a short flight of steps leads up from the brick-paved street to a doorway above.

BELOW: BUILD WITH WHATEVER COMES TO HAND

This seems to have been the motto of the builders of walls destined to be covered by stucco. The rich patina of age is revealed only when the building falls into disrepair.

BELOW: TURNING THE CORNER

Never much of a problem to ingenious Tuscan builders, even constructing a satisfactory junction for two walls presents itself as an opportunity for making an architectural statement.

Immediately inside this, a staircase ascends to the living quarters on the first floor. Each of these dwellings – they line countless streets all over Italy – is a little over 4 metres (12 feet) wide and 12 (about 50 feet) deep, with two rooms placed one behind the other on each of the two floors. The first-floor rooms were each lit by a single arched window placed front and back.

But wherever you are in Tuscany, whether among the chestnut woods or the wheatfields of the Casentino, or the vineyards in the tawny landscape of the Chianti, one of the most enduring features of the countryside is the *casa colonica*, the great farmstead around which all aspects of country life revolve. Here in the past the *fattoressa* – the farm manageress – cooked for the labourers, and here they would sleep during olive- and grape-picking time. Here the farming equipment was housed, the olives pressed and the oil and grain stored. The shape and size of the farmstead varies from one part of Tuscany to another, but its great bulk is always there, covered and protected by banks of terracotta pantiles. You see them in the works of the Renaissance artist Lorenzetti, whose peasants in paintings such as 'The Good Rule' are industriously tilling the fields surrounding the *case coloniche*.

This rural Tuscan idyll is today's country dreamland. Buy the *casa colonica*, do it up, then fill its kitchen with the fruits of the mushrooming cottage industries – tomato juice, vegetables in oil, salamis, smoked hams, jams and fruit preserves – all of which have been made in the manner of old. And yet attempts by wistful urban northerners to recreate it resound with hollow irony. The reality for the Tuscan *contadini*, the peasants, was the *mezzadria* system of farming whereby the landowner supplied a house, tools, seed and cattle, and the peasant the labour – both sharing the profits. At best it exploited the *contadini* mercilessly, forcing them into a subsistence existence; at worst it rendered them little more than serfs. But although pushed into the background, the quainter aspects of that other, older, Italy have not yet completely vanished.

In the 1960s, in some parts of the countryside, the rural population abandoned their homes and made for the cities. Finding themselves without workers, many landowners sold their farmhouses cheap to people from Milan and Rome, and to foreigners, as holiday homes. But

BELOW: BUILT TO ATTRACT BIRDS
It is not uncommon to find, around the upper edges of a dovecot, little landing stages for birds, put there to encourage them to move in to nest.

BELOW: THE MARK OF THE CRAFTSMAN
The doorposts and lintels on this old doorway still bear the scars of their maker's tools.

RIGHT: AT THE HEART OF COUNTRY LIFE
The casa colonica, *built around a more ancient construction, grows piecemeal with the result that roof pitches and gables face any which way.*

RIGHT: THE MEDIEVAL STREET SCENE
But for the electric cables, this street, like a great many others up and down the Tuscan countryside, is virtually unchanged since medieval times.

RIGHT: TOWN AND COUNTRY
Within the protective orbit of a nearby hill town, many a rural house was safe from marauding bands of cattle thieves and soldiers.

LEFT: THE VILLAGE WATCH
The close proximity of the hill towns did not necessarily mean they were amicably disposed to one another. Often they were sworn enemies, wreaking havoc in each other's fields.

while much of Tuscany is now farmed on a large, technically sophisticated scale and is far more specialized, with small factories for wine and olive oil, for salt, for sunflowers and strawberries, some land is still cultivated in a version of the *mezzadria* system. Here, *mezzadri* families remain – but only as 'part-time' farmers, since few could survive nowadays without a job in a local town or industry.

So, deep within the countryside, the old mixed farming system of vines, mulberry and olive trees on the hill slopes, of little patches of wheat, maize, cereals, legumes and forage, carries on. Even oxen harnessed to a plough testify to the survival of an ancient world. Binding vines, cutting the olives, chopping bamboo, using tools such as hand saws and axes – these are aspects of a time-honoured lifestyle based around the *casa colonica* with its rough stone walls, its great kitchen, its barns, its dovecot and its yard.

To outsiders, these modern *contadini* have it all ways: a healthy life living off the land, money in the bank, and a large, cool, roomy house rendered more appealing because of its great age. And from the security and comfort of their newly restored *casa colonica* – the old well filled with geraniums, the haylofts converted into bedrooms, the kitchen moved from the upper floor to a more convenient situation at ground level where the stables once were, terracotta oil jars now planted with herbs, swimming pool sparkling where vegetables and tomatoes were once planted in rows and watered with unfailing regularity – these English, French and German 'Tuscans' cannot fail to notice one of the most puzzling paradoxes of the Tuscan scene: the architectural style of the *casa colonica*, whose inhabitants lived at subsistence level against a backdrop of poverty and hardship, is often full of references to the Renaissance, the period that contains the roots of our civilization.

The Renaissance was the period in which, in Florence, Pisa, Siena and Lucca in the fourteenth and fifteenth centuries, there emerged a great deference for the traditions of Classical Antiquity and for its ideas and achievements. But, although bludgeoned almost into oblivion by the Dark Ages following the days of Ancient Rome, the spirit of Antiquity had never really left Tuscany. Even the rule of the Countess Mathilda (1076–1115), in which Tuscan Romanesque

BELOW: THE ANCESTRAL DOORWAY
The coat of arms points to the social standing of this small-town family. The great wooden doors announce security, confidence even, while the curtains are drawn against prying eyes on hot summer afternoons when the doors are left open.

RIGHT: THE PAINTERLY APPROACH
Simple painted decoration on stucco articulates the wall surface on the outside of this building.

RIGHT: OVER AND ABOVE
Often built in constricted sites, the houses of many Tuscan villages are built over alleyways. Here, a ceiling is made up of simple wooden beams on top of which are laid flat terracotta tiles, with brick arches supporting the buildings above.

architecture blossomed, was renowned for its Roman-mindedness long before the official era of the Renaissance (1300–1550). The difference between the Romanesque period and the Renaissance was that the former adhered strictly to the Classical tradition while the latter adapted what it knew of Antiquity to contemporary styles, so that Tuscan intellect and grace fused with Roman simplicity and poise.

Artists and architects strove to recreate the glorious age of Rome; and at the time the rural architecture of Tuscany, amongst the richest and most varied in Italy, benefited from this creative activity just as subsequent generations have done ever since.

While buildings quite naturally reflect their surroundings in terms of what materials were available locally – stone, slate, clay – the more important ones also owed stylistic allegiance to whatever artistic centre they were closest to. Consequently there are wide variations in style from one city to the next. A rural chapel or church in the orbit of Pisa in the twelfth or thirteenth century, for example, might have been decorated externally with striped 'zebra-work' panels of dark and light marble, a technique less common around Florence.

LEFT: THE RURAL IDYLL
An abandoned casa colonica *in Chianti, old fruit trees gradually encroaching on the vineyards and meadows surrounding it.*

Such differences are less astonishing when one remembers the ferocious rivalry that existed between these cities as each one tried to extend its influence, rivalry that often erupted into warfare, impeding trade and stemming the flow of building materials and the free travel of craftsmen from one place to the next.

While these variations are far more noticeable amongst great buildings — the cathedrals and the palaces — certain stylistic elements have filtered down from Florence or Pisa to the rural enclaves in their orbit: the design of a window surround or the shape of a loggia, the carving of an architrave or the outline of a roof, and the harmonious proportions and a sense of formality of even relatively humble buildings, with symmetrical arrangements of windows and doors. In most instances, this was simply a case of the peasants copying the building style of their peers.

This is particularly noticeable in the countryside near Florence, the great fount of ideas during the Renaissance period: farmhouses might have little arcaded loggias whose vaults spring from carved 'acanthus' corbels; there might be a portico; windows could be framed in stone, and topping the lintel of each there might be a cornice consisting of a cyma recta (a double-curved moulding, concave above and convex below). There might be a perfect square plan seven bays along with an entrance portal centrally placed in the fourth bay. All of these are in tune with the spirit of the Renaissance and consequently there is a Classical grace about even the remotest, lowliest *casa colonica* which lifts it from the dust of the fields and gives it dignity.

Some of the most conspicuously beautiful rural buildings in Tuscany are the *case coloniche* in the Chianti. This region to the north of Pienza and the Valdichiana, with its low undulating hills, lies at the heart of Tuscany. Its landscape matches many people's idea of what Italy ought to look like. Here the cypress trees march in rows up to the crests of the hills, and there are villas, castles, abbeys and farmhouses dotted about. But the strangest to look at are the latter, the *case coloniche*. Easily recognizable, they have a dominant tower-like projection at their core with the rest of the building, to which it is joined by a sloping roof, laid out around it on a roughly square plan. These buildings were very often constructed at the summit of a hill or

RIGHT: THE LOGGIA

The influence of the Renaissance can be seen even on the humblest farm building in Tuscany. Here, just outside Montalcino, the rough loggia of this farmhouse evokes that of a great country villa built during the Medici period. The farmhouse loggia enclosed a space in which work could continue unabated in extreme weather conditions; in the grander houses it was a cool, shady point from which to admire the view.

RIGHT: CENTURIES OF EXPANSION

Over the centuries this farmhouse, like countless others throughout Tuscany, has grown haphazardly, extended to fit the requirements of its occupants with whatever materials were to hand locally. This can be seen from the way the straight edges of former cornerstones butt up against expanses of wall added later. At the core of this building are the remains of a medieval tower house, its finely cut arched doorway still in place.

ABOVE: BRICK WITH STONE
This gothic church façade sports a meticulously restored pointed arch into which has been set a religious subject.

LEFT: POWER IN THE COUNTRYSIDE
A rustic castello *rises from the terraces of old olive trees. The martial face of late medieval Tuscany gradually gave way to a more gentle approach to life in the hills.*

ABOVE: VARIETY AND PATTERN
Variety in pattern, material and technique is accidental rather than intentional.

facing down a valley, and nowadays the tower portion is often transformed into a belvedere from which the occupants of the building can admire the surrounding landscape. In the attic region there was, and sometimes still is, a dovecot. Constructed as a loggia with, say, three small arches, the belvedere was also where the women of the house could work unhampered by unpleasant weather. Alternatively there may have been a loggia in the main body of the house, closer to the kitchen and the family rooms on the first floor and the barns and stables at ground level.

These buildings reflect the early history of this part of Tuscany as, from the tenth century, people began to move to the countryside from the cities. This was a slow process, hampered by the fact that the Tuscan countryside was anything but the sweet paradise it is nowadays. In fact, it was dangerous to venture far into it without proper protection.

In the warring Middle Ages, the landowner's house was a tall, block-built watch tower (such as the projection at the core of the *casa colonica*). An extremely simple building, it had a few very basic windows and no decoration other than perhaps an interesting archivolt at the entrance, or castellations around the top. Square in plan, it had a single room per floor, with the storeys connected by a wooden staircase. At a time of constant feuding between the Papal supporters, the Guelfs, and those of the Emperor, the Ghibellines, these towers were designed to keep the enemy faction out and the family and extended family in. The menace of constant attacks meant that the inhabitants of the villages dared not go out into the fields or to the woods because they would be robbed of their tools, or, on the way back from the mills, of their flour. Nothing was safe during this period, neither houses, mills, barns nor livestock.

Some idea of what these towers were like when they were built can be had from a visit to San Gimignano or Volterra. At one time such towers were fairly common in the towns of central Italy. In fact, in the thirteenth century San Gimignano was said to have had 76 (it now has only 15). Florence is supposed to have had 150, while in Lucca they are said to have 'risen like a forest'. As time went by the urban towers evolved into the private palaces that are such a feature of Italian city

RIGHT: PRIVATE WORSHIP
Attached to this farmhouse in the Chianti is a tiny chapel, perhaps more of a private shrine to a local saint – or the patron saint of the resident family – used on family occasions or on the saint's feast day.

RIGHT: TUSCANY AND THE TWENTIETH CENTURY
This scene, with casa padronale, *church and village houses, reflects the traditional social divisions of the countryside.*

LEFT: OGEE SURVIVOR

Although the ogee arches are still intact, possibly still as they were in the fourteenth century, the round relieving arches have been knocked away and large square windows placed in them. In these ancient town houses, pattern comes from the serried ranks of windows and the odd window detail.

LEFT: THE ROUGH AND THE SMOOTH

Juxtaposed against the clean-cut and very crisp incisions of the granite masonry on the right are rough stone walls. The former is imported stone, the latter a local material.

architecture today while, as the countryside became more civilized, the country towers were transformed into two other basic building types: the *villa-fattoria* and the *casa colonica*.

If the landowner continued to use the building as an occasional residence — either when he came to oversee the operations of his *contadini* during the harvest, or for holidays with his family during the summer months — it became what is known as a *villa-fattoria*. In some cases these, enlarged over the centuries, became quite grand. You see them now, part villa, part farmhouse, the main residence stuccoed, whitewashed and adorned perhaps with stone quoins. There might even be a *stemma*, a coat of arms testifying to the importance of the owner and his family, over the main door. Spread out beside it, or perhaps round the back, are the barns and outbuildings for farm use. In some cases the old towerhouse is still recognizable, incorporated into the later accretions as a 'feature'.

Some *ville-fattorie* simply developed into villas plain and simple. From Roman times, a villa had meant a country estate. In the Middle Ages this was conceived as a setting — inevitably with a garden — in which a man of culture could be at ease with his books, his thoughts and his friends. Having a country villa in the fifteenth century was a humanist ideal, and many an old castellated towerhouse was converted around this time, with gardens, loggias and porticoes.

Alberti, the Renaissance architectural theorist, suggested in his treatise *De re aedificatore* on the advice of the Romans Pliny the Younger and Vitruvius, that 'the ancients favoured making the portico facing south, so that in the summer when the sun traces a higher orbit, its rays should not enter, whereas in winter they should enter'. Such

RIGHT: BUILT, RE-BUILT AND RESTORED
A quaint, possibly reconstructed, entrance dating from the fifteenth century, this doorway bears the name and coat of arms of its original builders and owners.

RIGHT: THE ART OF THE RENAISSANCE
The design of the casa colonica *owes a great debt to the Renaissance. Handsome proportions give the house its character. In reality, it is a rough, simple farmhouse built on an embankment — hence the slanted wall and the great stone terrace in front of it.*

advice stimulated the occupants' sense of well-being and increased the arcadian mood so essential to the country villa ideal.

These villas did not belong only to the landowning nobility, however. As soon as a merchant became well off he invested money in farmland, often with a small villa to which he and his family would go in the summer. Not as grand perhaps as its aristocratic counterpart, it was nevertheless a smaller version of it and nowadays many such buildings can be seen scattered over the hills and slopes surrounding Florence and Siena. Rejuvenated for twentieth-century use, these are

RIGHT: RURAL ANTIQUITY
Hardly anything about this rural clutch of buildings – farm cottages, chapel and barns – points to the modern world. It is a timeless scene.

RIGHT: THE HEART OF THE FARM
This casa padronale *has a chapel attached to it which would have been used by farming families living too far from a town or village to attend church.*

the type usually restored and lived in today by non-farming people as holiday homes.

But if the seigneurial class chose not to inhabit their ancient abodes, they either abandoned them (and there are plenty still to be seen throughout Tuscany today), or gave them as bribes to the *contadini*. From this point on they began to acquire the characteristics of the *casa colonica*. More rooms were simply added on around them, and they grew and developed as the countryside was colonized and the agricultural system was reorganized – particularly at the beginning of the thirteenth century.

At this time there were technological improvements – mills, rotation of crops – which meant greater productivity. And with these came new 'units of production' called the *poderi* – patches of land on which the peasant workers had a house and where they farmed the land of the *mezzadrie*. By the fourteenth century this system of farming was widespread and by a century later so were the *case coloniche*, now one of the most enduring features of the Tuscan countryside.

LEFT: A TUSCAN FARMSTEAD
Part farmhouse, part stable and barn, the farmstead is one of the most characteristic sights of the Tuscan landscape. Bathed in the warm glow of late afternoon sunshine, with its pantiled roof and Mediterranean colours this one could be anywhere in Tuscany were it not for the open, prairie-like fields surrounding it. It is situated just outside Siena.

LEFT: TILES AND PANTILES
Houses the length and breadth of Tuscany are roofed with tiles and pantiles the same colour as their walls. Where the sirocco or mistral has been particularly successful in raising the roof, new tiles, held in place by rocks and stones, have replaced the old. Here traditional pantiles form the bulk of the roof covering while flat tiles are used at the edges.

LIGURIA

LIGURIA IS ONE OF the best known of Italy's fourteen regions. It is where many Italians — and foreigners — spend their summer holidays. The Italians, in particular the Milanese, make a rush for its coast when the heat in the cities becomes impossible to bear. And yet these holidaymakers rarely, if ever, venture into the region's interior. What attracts them are the resorts along the coastal Riviera di Levante and the Riviera di Ponente, respectively east and west of Genoa; this is summertime Liguria where the climate favours the growth of palms and oleanders, oranges and lemons, flowers and herbs.

This has been the pattern of the summer season ever since it first dawned on Italians, centuries ago, that life outside the city could be a pleasurable experience. All over Italy the so-called *villeggiatura* (the city-dweller's annual withdrawal to the countryside or seaside) has spawned a particular type of architecture. *Villeggiatura* was popularized by the Medici in Tuscany in the fifteenth century, though it was Petrarch, reviving a much more ancient idea in the mid-fourteenth century, who first suggested that the contemplative life, the life of artistic and philosophical creativity, could only blossom in the quiet of the countryside — to no avail, as it happens, because his contemporaries were interested in the country only as somewhere to rear livestock. Lining the coasts there are scores of large and small villas, some grand, others ordinary and undistinguished, waiting to absorb this flood of summer invaders.

Beyond the coastline of Liguria Nature seems, by contrast, to have hurled at the landscape as much vitriol as it could muster. The interior houses some of the least-known areas of northern Italy. The concept of *villeggiatura* is unheard of in this part of the world. Here, amongst the hostile peaks of the Maritime Alps and the Apennines, the stony ravines and the black gorges (black because the sun never reaches them), life is quiet and rustic. An empty and almost barren landscape, dotted only sparsely with hill towns and hamlets, is squeezed in

LEFT: TRIORA
This hill town was once an impenetrable stronghold, a mountain fastness from which its occupants could defend themselves from the five towers of its castle. Perched on the side of Monte Trono, it has an almost 360-degree view of the surrounding countryside.

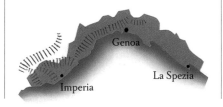

LEFT: COASTAL TAGGIA
Clambering up the side of the hill is an unruly mixture of humble and rather plain old stone houses and somewhat grander ones, the status of the latter underlined by their position at the brow of the incline. Plain colour wash makes up for the lack of external decoration.

LEFT: VERNAZZA
The blatant juxtaposition of features from different periods — the almost vertical medieval stone archway and the nineteenth-century window are very obvious clues to this building's history.

between the frontier of France, southern Piedmont and western Emilia-Romagna.

Accompanying these two Ligurias are two very distinct types of architecture. Each is a reflection of the lifestyle, and the history, of the zone in which it is found. One, the villa architecture already mentioned, is found almost exclusively along the coastline. The other, much more ancient than the first, consists of the tall, gaunt houses of the hill towns and villages and is confined mostly to the valleys and mountain peaks of the interior. The one is light-hearted and festive — one of Liguria's most memorable characteristics. The other is dour, watchful and secretive. Its nearest equivalents are the buildings of the Umbrian and Tuscan hill towns, though the buildings of rural Liguria are far less gentle and beguiling and have none of the radiance associated with the terracotta-coloured settlements of central Italy.

To have two such different architectures with virtually nothing in between — except in the modern outskirts of the bigger cities — might seem rather strange to an outsider. But the region's history and topography provide the key to this. The story of Liguria, at least

LEFT: PORTOFINO
The houses of this little seaside port are distinguished from one another only because they vary in height and colour. A semblance of individuality creeps in where painted bands separate the various storeys. At pavement level, shops and vaulted storage chambers open directly to the outside through arches or simple doors. These are humble artisans' or fishermen's houses.

outside Genoa, is not a particularly happy one. Genoa has always been the powerhouse of this region because of its location on the Via Aurelia, the main coast road to France. Competing with Venice, it was in a strong position to connect this area to the ports of the Levant. Consequently, like the merchants of Venice, the Genoese grew wealthy transporting Crusaders to the Holy Lands in the twelfth and thirteenth centuries. In the Middle Ages, when it was a powerful maritime republic, Genoa began to extend its influence over the surrounding territory, facing what turned out to be rather strenuous resistance from rural feudal barons who ran the interior much as they liked. For and against Genoa, against one another, and against the continual harassment by the Saracen pirates (Muslims from north Africa who also plagued the south coast of France, Sicily and other parts of Italy's west coast) from the sea, the hill towns of the interior, only a short distance inland from the coast, began to acquire their defensive characteristics. Even as late as the sixteenth century, while the Genoese merchant princes were adorning the coasts within the protective arms of Genoa with villas, the towns of the interior were battening down the hatches in resistance to the hated Saracens who destroyed their crops, looted churches, raped the women and made off with their cattle.

While the hill towns remained inert, locked away in a rugged and infertile countryside, the coastal towns blossomed. The most conspicuous examples of the coastal villa architecture are those dating from the eighteenth and, predominantly, the nineteenth centuries. They can be seen around the big resort towns of San Remo, Rapallo, La Spezia (names which summon up images of immense casinos, roulette tables, floor shows and the aroma of exotic flowers) and Genoa itself, and around fashionable smaller resorts like Portofino (where the likes of the Agnelli and the Pirelli holiday) and Santa Margherita Ligure. Straddling the undulating coastline in an almost continuous ribbon, these seaside villas were – and generally still are – the setting for a slow, easy life dedicated to leisure. Then as now they tend to be used only in the summer, the traditional period of the *villeggiatura*.

Some of these buildings stand in the shelter of hidden coves and rocky inlets, on occasions inaccessible except from the sea. Others are on tiny private peninsulas thick with oleanders and pines. Their gardens are small but rich and semi-tropical, with formal cut hedges, statues and terraces. There are balconies with ornate railings and balustrades overlooking the Mediterranean.

Surprise and variation are the key to the design: anything from a neo-Classical mansion to a neo-Gothic or Moorish villa or even a castellated house mimicking the real thing further inland is possible. Genoa is responsible for having produced this very special 'Tyrrhenian' type of maritime villa which, historically, has shown an enchanting and eclectic blend of various ornamental motifs. Nowadays these have been bastardized and it is not unusual to find incrustation – like facings of gleaming marble – from Tuscany, window surrounds from Piedmont, and richly decorated loggia arcades from Venice and Lombardy all on the same building. Many have a Moorish note added to their designs which, just like the Oriental-style buildings of Venice, is as much a result of the region's historic maritime connections with the Levant. Genoa's fifteenth-century Palazzo Doria, for example, and other buildings like it, are a bridge between the original models of the

RIGHT: MIX AND MATCH
Trompe l'oeil *is always cheaper than the real thing, especially if marble for architectural detailing is not available locally. On these two neighbouring houses at Santa Margherita Ligure on the Ligurian coast, 'broken' window pediments, balustrading and other architectural finery are painted rather than carved on to the façades. Paint gives the artist a freer rein and allows the owners to assert their individuality; each house is different.*

RIGHT: CAMOGLI
The Ligurian coastline has long been a favourite watering hole for both the Italians and the British. Brightly painted villas, many of them dating from the end of the nineteenth century, are dotted about amongst the tangle of exotic trees and plants – pines, palms and eucalyptus. Their design is governed by fantasy; it is not unusual to see a 'Moorish' house on one side of a Renaissance-style palace and a 'Gothic' folly on the other.

RIGHT: ST GEORGE
VANQUISHES THE DRAGON

The patron saint of England turns up at Portofino where, it is said, his bones were left by passing Crusaders returning to Italy from the Holy Land. Here he frequently appears in a frescoed panel on the façade of a village house, a saintly intercessor between the occupants and the Almighty.

RIGHT: VILLAS AT SANTA MARIA LIGURE

If you cannot afford the real thing, then why not go for the painted version? Richly adorned, frescoed façades are just as magnificent as those studded with real marbles, statues and carvings. These lesser mansions carefully imitated their grander counterparts in a technique that is rarely seen today.

Orient and the nineteenth-century adaptations that survive on villas along the Ligurian coast.

And there are, of course, less imposing – even small – variations on these themes where the lack of adornment is made up for with the use of vivid colour washes. However, in this part of Liguria small is not necessarily a sign of diminished beauty or even of moderate means. Far from it, as the example of Portofino shows. Here the coastal slopes are so steep that big houses are simply impractical. Even those cannily sited on a natural ledge or terrace are fairly modest, perhaps one room deep. And yet Portofino is one of the most expensive stretches of real estate in Italy, if not in Europe, frequented by industrial magnates, deposed royalty and film stars, all of whom, if not staying in one of Portofino's hotels, must squeeze into a small two-storey *villino* for a share of this idyllic stretch of Italy.

Whatever their form nowadays, these villas are descended from the splendid *ville suburbane* (suburban villas) built in the sixteenth century for Genoa's merchant princes on the outskirts of their city. The best known – and the most magnificent – were those designed by the

LEFT: THE ART OF ARTIFICE

The window surrounds, doorcase and quoins of this nineteenth-century villa, well maintained and carefully painted, are made of stucco. Painted a different colour from the façade, their function is not just decorative. Rather, they give definition to the shape of the building.

LEFT: HEIGHT AND DIGNITY

Copious use of stucco and paint enlivens the façade of this palazzo *in San Remo, Liguria. Vertical bands, pilaster-like, give height, while the horizontal stringcourses above and below the windows give dignity.*

architect Galeazzo Alessi and Giovanni Angelo Montorsoli, a sculptor (and a pupil of Michelangelo's) for whom architecture was only a secondary interest. Their work was prolific, providing the prototypes for villas which prolonged the splendour of the city far along the Ligurian coastline.

The point about the Ligurian coast was, as the seventeenth-century writer and diarist, John Evelyn, once remarked, that 'there was little or no extent of ground' on which to build. So the architects had to be doubly ingenious in planning and siting their buildings on the narrow ledges of rock on the slopes of leafless, dusty hills.

But why make all this effort? One of the reasons must surely have been that just like today an 'outlook' was a covetable possession and that all the architectural features that went with it – terraces, loggias, balconies and so on – were hugely attractive and appealing. Gardens were necessarily small and filled with sculpture rather than with the water and greenery of their counterparts in contemporary Rome and Florence. These houses were Genoa's pleasure palaces, the 'ravishing retirements of the Genoese nobility', as Alessi remarked.

LEFT: MEDIEVAL SURVIVORS
Hill towns and villages are strewn along the upper reaches of Liguria's barren valleys, their roofs sloping with the incline of the hillsides, their houses and churches the colour of the local stone. Each house is joined to the next, mimicking a defensive, protective wall. From below they appear to be half house, half fortress.

Rich in detail and ornament (mural paintings and stucco), lined with marble, and fitted with graceful loggias and airy colonnades, the most characteristic of this type and of this period had roof balustrades, a richly carved frieze and cornice – or at the very least an elaborately painted one – and niches fitted with statues and marble benches. The terraces, also laid with marble in geometric patterns, were edged by more balustrades and connected to one another by broad, shallow flights of steps.

Lesser mansions had their architectural decoration (always real on their grander counterparts) painted on to their stuccoed external façades. Often this ran even to colonnades of Ionic or fluted Corinthian columns for the upper storeys and perhaps rusticated pilasters for those on the bottom level or facing the street. These *faux* exteriors were then adorned with statues and other ornaments painted entirely in monochrome in a series of greys, a technique called *grisaille*. This painting of architectural ornament on to buildings is very characteristic of Genoese architecture (it can be seen up and down the coast even in humble portside homes of fishermen as, for example, at Portofino and Camogli), and was done with such skill that, from not too far away, it is often impossible to distinguish a genuine architectural projection from a frescoed counterfeit.

Common to all the *villeggiatura* bolt holes, and particularly to their modern equivalents, was a feeling for luxury. This is perhaps the whole essence of their character. The builders of these villas were searching for tranquillity and peace of mind, an escape from ordinary routines and the affairs of the city.

Areas of whimsy are common to the design of holiday villas wherever they may be. Freeing themselves of social conformities, architects and patrons felt able to be more indulgent than would normally have been the case in the city. This is something in which Leone Battista Alberti, the Renaissance architect and architectural theorist, expressed an interest in the mid-fifteenth century. He was aware of a hierarchy of traditional values associated with varying types of architecture in which the villa was towards the bottom of the pile, the urban palace and civic architecture near the top, and ecclesiastical architecture at the apex. Acknowledgement of this by the great Alberti

BELOW: SAINTLY INTERCESSORS
These beautiful lintels, adorned with saints and religious imagery, acquired during lulls in the turmoil, offered much-needed comfort to the inhabitants. Carved from stone, they are often the only external decoration that a house has.

gave even the most wayward villa design credibility, thus innovation and variety have been – and are – more important in villa design than in any other significant type of architecture.

This goes a long way to explain the flights of fantasy and the eclectic ranges of style manifest on a single building in the coastal suburbs of Genoa. In addition to this, detached on their own small neighbouring plots, there are often more disparate styles here than anywhere else in the country with very strangely exotic oddities cheek by jowl: Gothic-Moorish horror houses, all ogee arches and terracotta incrustation, alongside Art Nouveau houses dripping in foliage, painted, stuccoed or wrought in iron. From Liguria to Naples, Palermo to Apulia, wherever the holidaying Italian public made popular a stretch of coastline, the story is the same albeit on a less dramatic scale.

Liguria's 'other' architecture consists of a variety of isolated, rustic buildings: mills, remote hamlets way up on the highest peaks of the Ligurian Alps and accessible only by donkey or on foot; chapels and wayside shrines (simple stone pediments above a niche containing a faded fresco or nowadays a plastic Madonna); and the wood-framed bothies clad in thatch of the woods of the Val di Vara. Each one reflects its immediate environment in terms of the materials used (slate, granite blocks, limestone, wood), and the shape, size and use to which it is put. Some were – still are – seasonal places, in particular the little hamlets where the shepherds take their sheep to graze in the summer. Here, in the rough little stone cottages, they live on home-made ricotta and what their families might bring them from home in the hill towns way down in the valley below. In the winter these seasonal hamlets are shuttered and empty, though nowadays most are simply abandoned altogether. They have simply outlived their usefulness. Their owners have drifted away to the coastal towns to lead very different lives from their ancestors who will have passed these buildings (their most valued possession apart from the family goat and the smallholding down in the valley, crammed with olive trees and a few scraggy vineyards) down from one generation to the next.

There are also the tall, stone houses of the region's ragged hill towns. Perched at the head of a valley with a good all-round view of the surrounding territory, the buildings of the hill towns shoulder each

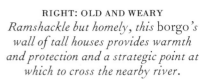
RIGHT: OLD AND WEARY
Ramshackle but homely, this borgo's wall of tall houses provides warmth and protection and a strategic point at which to cross the nearby river.

ABOVE: TAGGIA AND ITS GENTRY
The family stemma, *or coat of arms, gives a certain dignity to this simple doorway. Carved from local stone, it is a much revered relic, and is often the only pointer to a family's former illustrious position.*

ABOVE: MIX AND MATCH
All over Italy, buildings are repaired using whatever comes to hand. Here, Roman bricks, old stone lintels still bearing the marks of their makers, re-used stones and slate are brought together in this restored wall.

LEFT: APRICALE

Apricale, like many of the hill towns in the remote recesses of Liguria's Maritime Alps, seems to have been poured down the side of the hill on which it stands. From below it appears to be half fortress, half town, the houses and church welded together around dank alleys and vaulted passages. Earthquakes, brutal pirate raids and oppressive rule by feudal barons combined to give these hill towns their present distinctive appearance.

other protectively as they peer down the slopes in fearful anticipation of attacks from bands of marauders. The wretchedness and tension that this must have engendered in the daily lives of their inhabitants is written all over the buildings. It was hardly ever possible to build outside the confines of the town's protective outer limits. You did so at your own risk. Consequently the Ligurian countryside is virtually empty except for what has been built during the last fifty years or so and the dry stone walls of the terraces cut into the hillsides long ago in order to grow olive trees and vines.

The more frequent the battering sustained by the inhabitants of rural Liguria, the greater the impetus towards a defensive style of building. Seen from below, these peculiarly inward-looking houses are not so much individual buildings as continuous masses of masonry. The intention was to protect the inhabitants of the town *en masse* first, and the residents of the individual compartments second. So the outer houses are presented to onlookers below as a continuous protective town wall, one that has apparently been randomly punctured by small

BELOW, LEFT AND RIGHT: INSECURE AND DEFENSIVE

The watchful nature of Liguria's rural towns and villages is overwhelming. Tiny, mean windows and rough-shod walls, often built of stones taken from some Roman fortification, underline the defensive preoccupations of their inhabitants. Narrow, cobbled alleys and streets, particularly those tunnelled beneath the buildings, have never been washed down by the rain. Few see the light of day – in fact, most are permanently dark from lack of sunshine.

BELOW: ARCHITECTURAL RELIC
*Only occasionally is there a carved
detail of some kind to adorn the
exterior of an otherwise plain Ligurian
village building. Here, a medieval
carved capital, undoubtedly moved
from some other building, pretends to
hold up the lintel of the window.*

RIGHT: USED AND RE-USED
*Once a civic building, this is now a
tenement. Dignified arcades have been
filled in and are now used as bedroom
extensions. When space is at a
premium, as it is in practically every
Ligurian town and village, then
ingenuity is the great provider.*

square, blank openings for windows. The only distinction between one person's property and the next one's was the colour of the shutters on these windows.

Even today, most of these mountain citadels are virtually impregnable: a narrow winding road creeps up to a gateway, passes it, then burrows into a tight mass of buildings, each house towering fortress-like overhead. The climb from the outer limits to the top of the town is a steep and tortuous one through cobbled, vaulted tunnels, alleys and passages. The buildings are stepped up the hillsides, most having only a single-pitched slate or pantiled roof, the slope falling away in the direction of the fall of the land. Unlike Venetian buildings, chimney stacks are low and inconspicuous. Entrances open directly on to the street, or are connected to it by short flights of stone steps beneath which cavernous cellars housed – and in very many cases continue to house – livestock.

Plain and mostly unadorned, these are rough, basic buildings with street surface, wall and roof made of the same materials. There were simply no means with which to provide the buildings with decorative adornments other than the occasional whitewash on stucco façade. Only very occasionally is there a relief carving – a date or the image of a saint – above a door. In the eyes of the inhabitants, saintly intervention was very often the only thing, apart from a stout defensive wall, that might have protected them from calamity.

Part of the fascination of these places, however, is not to look for surface adornment in the accepted sense – ornamental stucco, wall painting and architectural ornamentation. Instead, notice the almost infinite variety of uses to which the rough local stone has been put.

Poverty is often the source of great ingenuity. It mixes practicality with expediency, a functional beauty the by-product: over doors and windows, up-ended vertical and near-vertical flat stones are embedded in the wall of building blocks laid in horizontal strata to form a relieving arch; there is infill and repair, big stones and small blocks, rubble and slate; there are large, flat, precisely cut stones (and on occasions wood) for lintels and door posts still criss-crossed by the marks of the cutter's tools; large thin slabs are used as treads on steps beneath which the 'risers' are a mass of tightly packed rubble; buttress

arches, pointed or flat-rounded, soar overhead steadying the buildings; sometimes there are patterns in the cobblestones, and directional variations in the blocks of the vaults of the tunnels and passages. There is rhythm, contrast, texture and pattern everywhere you look: but it is coarse and uneven. It is there by accident rather than by design. Often the stones and blocks that make up these buildings were used just as they came out of the ground. Unsurprisingly, seen from below, the buildings of rural Liguria seem to be welded to, or to grow from, the rock on which they stand.

The inhabitants of these places are still mostly very poor, able to afford only marginal alterations to the dwellings their ancestors built. Any change in their fortunes has to be sought in the large towns on the coast; and it is for this reason that so many of these little hill-top enclaves are today empty and in part abandoned. Their inhabitants have fled to an easier life, returning perhaps only at weekends or on local feast days to air out the rooms of their former homes. And perhaps the only happy consequence of this is that very many of Liguria's hill settlements are in their original state and still, by and large, medieval in appearance.

LEFT: RHYTHM, TEXTURE AND COLOUR
Even the simplest façade has something of interest about it. Here it is the rhythm. Banks of shuttered windows set the pace, while the contrasting textures of rough and smooth stucco work provide visual relief in what might otherwise seem a rather monotonous façade.

LEFT: THE LAST RESORT
Often the rocky Ligurian coastal hill-terraces are too narrow to support buildings, so on any reasonably flat patch of land, no matter how inhospitable the location, a village inevitably springs up. Here the houses are crammed together around a little inlet. A castle on the seaward side protects the village both from the wind and against invasion from the sea.

UMBRIA

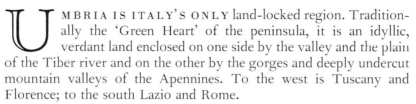

UMBRIA IS ITALY'S ONLY land-locked region. Traditionally the 'Green Heart' of the peninsula, it is an idyllic, verdant land enclosed on one side by the valley and the plain of the Tiber river and on the other by the gorges and deeply undercut mountain valleys of the Apennines. To the west is Tuscany and Florence; to the south Lazio and Rome.

The plain of the Tiber river is in the greatest possible contrast to the blue-green hills and steep upland valleys that characterize the bulk of this region. The one is well inhabited and bristling with activity, the other is relatively empty and silent. Its remoteness and inaccessibility keep it this way. There is the odd farmstead or lone towerhouse hugging the fringe of a forest or peering cautiously over the brow of a hill, or the occasional hill town or village clinging to a crag. But these are outposts where the pace of life is slow and unchanging.

Umbria has a lyrical fascination which is quite at odds with its violent history. Perhaps best known as the home of St Francis of Assisi, and the spiritual retreat of a whole host of other religious figures including Clare and Valentine, little has changed in Umbria, the region where once these saints perceived most acutely the work of their Creator. In the paintings of the Umbrian School – the works of Piero della Francesca, Perugino or Pinturicchio – which can be seen in any number of churches and sanctuaries up and down the countryside, Umbria's gentle hills, splattered with soft, translucent light, form the background to works of religious inspiration reflecting a meditative, almost mystical landscape.

But Umbria's history is anything but mystical. The defensive character of the rural towns and villages, and often of the individual houses in them, is proof enough of this. The earliest peoples to inhabit the area were the Samnite and Umbrian tribes (according to Pliny, the latter were the oldest of all the Italian races). Long before the Romans marched in from their seven hills in ancient Latium, and before even the mysterious Etruscans had made their way to what eventually

LEFT: IZZALINI
Much of Umbria's early history was of war and battle. This borgo, *with its lookout tower, is a tenacious survivor from the Middle Ages. Stone-built, it gradually fell into disuse as the countryside was made safer. Now it is used as a dovecot.*

Perugia
Lake Trasimeno

RIGHT: SPELLO
Beneath the houses are storerooms, barns, woodstores and byres. Ancient cobblestones lead the way to a front door which is distinguished from the barns around it only by its smaller size. Just inside the door, narrow steps lead up to the living rooms on the first floor.

RIGHT: IN THE STYLE OF
THE RENAISSANCE
The most characteristic feature of the Umbrian landscape: the hill town. Plain, simple village houses are dominated by an elegant mansion, once the administrative centre of the surrounding countryside. The style of its windows — even its proportions — points to a knowledge of the architectural style of the Renaissance which emanated from Florence in the fifteenth century.

became a part of Etruria, these tribes found themselves faced with two choices: to settle on the valley bottoms amongst the rivers, lakes and bogs (eventually drained by the Romans) where the land was fertile but life was unsafe, or to make for the impregnable security of remote crags where the hilly slopes were suited only to subsistence cultivation. They chose the latter and the subsequent chaotic history of Umbria ensured that their descendants remained there, venturing out of their walled enclaves only to cultivate the land in their immediate vicinity. The crumbling terraces of old olives and vineyards surrounding some of the hill towns must date in part from this time.

Throughout the Dark Ages Umbria was a battlefield. After the fall of the Roman Empire when all semblance of order vanished, the region was crushed beneath waves of plundering Goths, Huns and Lombards, its inhabitants succumbing to plague, famine and poverty. Finally in the eighth century AD the Franks were invited by Pope Stephen III to come and restore some kind of peace to the region. Subsequently, the rulers of the Frankish Empire, Pepin the Short and then his son Charlemagne, brought order to this troubled part of Europe but on

LEFT: SANTA RESTITUTA

At the bottom of everyone's field or allotment stands a barn, or an outhouse, built from local stone. Here a wooden lintel supports the stone of the wall over the door. Apart from the cut stone for the door posts and the little regular opening for the pigeons, the rest of this building is roughly constructed.

Charlemagne's death Umbria, and much of the rest of Italy, was again plunged into chaos as powerful rival families sought to establish control. A central authority was missing and anarchy and internecine warfare flourished. Any towns unable to withstand the rigours of constant siege and invasion were simply abandoned or destroyed, their place taken by fortified villas and castles.

And so developed the most characteristic feature of the Umbrian landscape: hill towns, often of unimaginable antiquity, and the fortified *borghi*, the village-castles, perched out of harm's way up on some lonely rocky outcrop, rather than out in the open countryside. Each hill town was a self-sufficient community, the larger ones becoming first the economic and then the administrative centres of the countryside around them. Secular building took place on an unprecedented scale, giving the rapidly expanding towns the appearance that many of them still have today.

Each commune coveted the power and the territory of its neighbour. Neighbouring fiefdoms, Machiavellian in outlook and prone to forming bewilderingly complicated and short-lived alliances, fought each other on behalf of their nominal masters the Emperor (the Ghibelline faction) and the Pope (the Guelf faction), swapping allegiance as the mood took them, fuelling the confusion. Not surprisingly the countryside outside the town walls was a dangerous place to be: people ventured out to farm only when the coast was clear. Communications were also appalling: trade was impossible except between neighbouring towns – and even this seemed pointless since most were constantly at each other's throats.

All over Umbria ancient towerhouses survive, a testimony to the unpredictability of the times. Peering suspiciously out over the terraced hillsides, with a single entrance at ground level and just two rooms within, one above the other, connected by a wooden staircase, their role was primarily defensive: an easily defendable refuge against the bands of mercenaries who roamed the countryside. They could also be used as seasonal dwellings during the harvest should the farmer's plot of land be far from his home in the local town. Others were later adapted and extended to become farmhouses, easily recognizable because they are always the tallest part of the complex.

BELOW: MEDIEVAL MONTEFALCO
A pointed-arched medieval doorway leads to a storeroom. In the past it would have led to a dwelling or chapel. Perhaps it survives because it was covered-up, hidden from view by plaster rendering.

BELOW: MEDIEVAL MONTEFALCO
A pointed-arched medieval doorway leads to a storeroom. In the past it would have led to a dwelling or chapel. Perhaps it survives because it was covered-up, hidden from view by plaster rendering.

By the middle of the seventeenth century Umbria had fallen to the Papacy; for the next 250 years the province nodded off quietly, a slumbering, inactive backwater. By then, however, people had begun to move down into the Tiber Valley to farm the *prati*, the fields, stretched out in a purple-brown haze on its fertile floor. Nowadays this is the most highly populated part of Umbria. The *prati* are chequered with little parcels of land called the *poderi*, dotted with *case coloniche* and villas, and criss-crossed with tracks, lines of cypresses, vineyards, olive groves and fields.

The system of farming used in the *prati* (and elsewhere in the region where farming was possible) was that of the *mezzadria*. As in Tuscany it locked the peasant tenant farmers, the *contadini*, into a relationship with their landlords which could never be profitable — except for the latter. They cultivated their land on the landowner's estate in return for a share of the crops.

At one time the *contadino*'s whole livelihood was concentrated on his patch; it was an intensively cultivated patch where rent was paid to the landlord in the form of land upkeep, a percentage of the crops, transport to the granary and a half of the vet's fees. It was a tough subsistence lifestyle, though perhaps easier here on the plain than in the hills and Apennine valleys where very often the *contadini* would have to trek to work in rocky fields far from their homes. The rural homesteads of Umbria reflect this land-bound life: each building is reduced to the very basics and built of whatever materials were to hand locally. Survival was the key, which is why so much of a *casa colonica* is given over to storage and manufacture rather than to actual living space.

Umbria is still very much a 'peasant' economy in that some of what is produced on the *podere* ends up on the smallholder's own table with surplus being sold at the local market. Because of this, everything — beans, Jerusalem artichokes, peas, celery, onions — is organically grown; not as the result of some current trendy fad that the *signora* read about in a magazine but simply because methods of farming have changed so little over the centuries. Methods of wine-making in these areas, and very possibly the end product as well, are very similar to those described by Virgil in the *Georgics*.

RIGHT: CHANGE AND REPAIR AT SPELLO
Years of repair and change have left their mark on Italy's ancient buildings. Medieval houses, part brick but mostly stone, are still in use — a tribute to the skills of their builders all those centuries ago.

LEFT: GATEWAY TO PISSIGNANO

Beyond the gate of this little borgo, *a cobbled path leads up between the stone cottages and barns to the top of the village. At the centre of the path, strips of stone or brick provide a welcome foothold for a donkey laden with goods. They also provide a drainage gulley for rainwater.*

LEFT: PROTECTRESS OF THE HOUSEHOLD

A religious picture, squeezed into this opening on the wall of a house in Amelia, is graciously framed in marble.

LEFT: LOST GLORY
Pissignano grips the side of the hill, watching protectively over the plain below, its lookout towers — evidence of its former might — placed at intervals along the perimeter of the curtain wall. Once impenetrable, this little place is now an insignificant village filled with restored cottages.

LEFT: ANYTHING GOES
Built in the Middle Ages, these pointed arches have been sealed up, opened, then partially closed once again — and the basic structure is still in use today.

Another happy side effect of the tenacious grip on the old ways is that it is not unusual to see, say, a sixteenth-century *casa colonica* still used practically as intended when it was first built. A real *casa colonica* would have maybe three generations of the same family of farmers working and living in it. Life inside revolves, as it always has done, around the kitchen and more particularly the hearth —a great dugout along one wall, big enough for a man to stand in and dominated by a heavy mantelpiece. Black with years of soot, in centuries past it would have clanked with old hooks carrying kettles and wrought-iron arms carrying pots, and there would have been ancient blackened fire dogs to support the burning logs. The fire would have burned continuously. Most have succumbed to modernization now, marble replacing their old stone floors and electric cookers in place of the primitive arrangements in the flames.

The layout of these ancient domestic interiors varies considerably from house to house, but throughout Italy the kitchen has two essential fixtures; a *cassettina*, a little cupboard, in the wall beside the fireplace in which to keep the salt dry and under lock and key; and a terracotta washing basin set into the wall or sitting on a wooden frame in one corner of the room. The kitchen was almost always placed above the quarters for the animals and approached via an outside stone staircase, which might be covered. Low, dusty, terracotta-coloured, these old buildings, shambling across their patch of land, are sometimes attached to barns piled with hay and packed with carts and tractors of various vintages.

One wall or gable of the barn might be pierced with a zone of little openings, edged with baked tiles arranged in patterns, to better aerate the crops stored there. This is one of the few parts of a *casa colonica* that ever receives any decoration and the patterns and designs are often disarmingly simple. One other decorative area is the *forno*, the oven, for making the household bread. Its design and location vary from place to place: near Trevi you might find it halfway up the outside steps sheltered by a loggia so that work at it was unencumbered by the rain; near Umbertide it might be gouged from an outside wall, a sort of walk-in affair where the chimney is disguised as the pilaster of the loggia above; near Spoleto it might open out of the kitchen itself, added on like a separate room, its roof a strange dome-like construction rather like a miniature mosque.

Below the house the undercrofts, the paint peeling from their huge double wooden doors, are occupied by cattle, and there are outbuildings filled with stacks of brushwood, sacks and dusty glass bottles. And the grandmothers, clad in black, sit where they've always sat: in the shade of a simple covered, arched loggia, nodding off in the heat as they shell the peas or mutter to the chickens scrabbling about the cobbles.

In the cellars, with their ancient stone-flagged floors, there are great wooden casks for wine and possibly a wine press as well, bottled fruit and salamis, terracotta jars blackened with age and huge glass demi-johns for olive oil. Here, too, in a much venerated position, is the olive press: in some cases, apart from the buildings themselves, this is the oldest thing on site. Oil, a most precious commodity, is the staple of most small farms: the average Italian family can consume up to 40 or 50 litres (9 to 11 gallons) of oil a year and there is an old saying that he who is without olive trees is indeed a poor man.

RIGHT: ON GUARD AT SPELLO
A stout pair of polygonal towers guards the entrance to Spello – clear evidence of the defensive character of Umbria's towns and villages. By contrast, the houses which the wall and gates protect are simple, rather benign-looking structures.

Nowadays work on smallholdings such as these is rarely geared to subsistence farming as once it was, although the remnants of the *mezzadria* system of farming the land survive here and there. But now most of the *contadini* have themselves become *padroni*; total subservience to the *mezzadria* system never afforded anyone a new TV, or a washing machine, or a holiday by the sea. At least one member of the family, if not the patriarch himself, will have another job in town, farmwork being the preserve of his wife or his mother or even his mother-in-law, both of whom probably live on the *podere*. He himself will continue the pruning, watering the tomatoes, making bonfires and digging the water drainage channels at the weekends and each evening after work until the sun goes down. Sadly, the younger generation regards this kind of life, even in its mutant form, as anachronistic and it is not unusual to find the old family *casa colonica* divided into different parts – one for the depleted farming family, one for the foreign visitors and one for the absentee weekender who lives in Rome. This pattern is increasing all over Umbria, Tuscany and the Marche, but the one

RIGHT: THE BLIND EYE
A blind window is highlighted by the stucco which stops dramatically just short of obliterating it altogether. The little covered opening, with its stone structure, is medieval – or perhaps even earlier – while the door surround dates from a few centuries later.

RIGHT: DERUTA
This nineteenth-century house, as well as its earlier neighbour to the left, makes full use of the town's local industry – the manufacture of ceramic tiles and pottery. The tiles enrich the window surrounds and provide a frieze where paint or stucco might normally be used.

BELOW: BRICK AND STONE
A neat brick arch above the window provides a very pleasing contrast, both visually and aesthetically, to the all-enveloping stone of the rest of the building.

BELOW: BRICK AND STONE
A neat brick arch above the window provides a very pleasing contrast, both visually and aesthetically, to the all-enveloping stone of the rest of the building.

obvious benefit derived from it is that buildings are in good repair, often restored under the watchful eye of the local council ever conscious of the region's building heritage.

The great age of buildings, and the fact that little has been done over the centuries to alter their appearance, is perhaps the most impressive thing about the houses in rural Umbria. The reason for this was, quite simply, poverty: why waste precious cash on an ephemeral door surround if you are hard-pushed even to find enough bread and olives to feed the family? Not surprisingly, many rural villages and towns in Umbria are still medieval in appearance from one end to the other. Remove the cars, switch off the electric lights and you could be back in the Umbria of six hundred years ago. And it is not just the houses that have retained their old character. Narrow alleys squirming their way up the hill under stone-vaulted passages, or between the thick defensive walls of houses squeezed close together, have often escaped being covered in tarmac and concrete kerbstones and their cobbles are intact. Abutting these, seemingly continuous walls of masonry signify the presence of half a dozen houses, each one opening directly on to the street, a main entrance often marked out by a distinctive pattern in the cobbles in front of it.

In addition to this, if their houses were towerhouses, most Umbrian hill towns have a distinctly defensive character, easily maintainable, as at Postignano near Sellano. From each house tiny square windows watch the countryside, the bigger ones, arched at the top or square, placed near the top of the building; the smaller ones, if any, lower down. They scarcely reflect the layout of the building's rooms on the other side of the wall. In fact some rooms did not even have windows at all, and the uncomfortable, not to mention unhygienic, conditions this arrangement must have produced cannot have been particularly pleasant. For the most part, the layout of ordinary town and village houses was very simple indeed and remained unchanged for centuries: main living rooms, one maybe two, on the first floor; brick-vaulted stables and cellars at ground level, the latter hollowed out of the hillside at the back of the building, admirably suited to cool storage of oil and salamis. The upper levels – sometimes as at Postignano, where some houses have six storeys in all, there was more than one – have

RIGHT: IZZALINI
This picturesque idyll belies the fierce motives for its construction in the Middle Ages. Watchtower, church and huddle of houses, all built from the same grey local stone, are quite at odds with the rural tranquillity of the twentieth century.

The various elements of this façade are picked out in different materials: shaped wedges of stone form the arch of the door, while the uprights on either side are single, large stones capped by fired terracotta bricks.

high, beamed ceilings and floors of brick and stone and, if built on a slope, were entered via a side alley straight into the kitchen on the first floor.

At the top of the building, the attics contained, and still contain, the dovecots which the birds entered from little openings just below the eaves. Often these are the most highly adorned areas of a building; it is as if the builders imagined that even a modicum of decoration would entice the birds in. There are rows of little circular apertures in the outside wall, each one lined and criss-crossed with terracotta tiles. In other buildings there are triangular openings or square ones with carved lintels. In one case, on a dovecot at Protte near Spoleto, birds have been colourfully frescoed on to the wall just above the opening as if flying towards it. And dotted about the wall at attic level there are often little ledges for the birds to rest on.

Throughout Umbria rural houses have often been owned by the same family for generations. The houses simply grew organically, added to as each generation desired, although in the cramped confines of Umbria's hill towns and villages there was nowhere to extend but heavenwards. The narrowness of the houses in places like Postignano makes them highly unsuitable for modern living: whereas in the past the whole family would have been content to share a large bed curtained off from the kitchen on the floor above the stables, the domestic requirements of the twentieth century, even at the humblest level, are not easily adaptable to houses which only have a single room per floor. It is difficult nowadays to find a house in which the original arrangement remains.

But the texture of the region's rural houses, wherever they are located, is timeless. The materials for building – for making bricks, tiles, and stone for lintels and floors, the cobbles for pavements, and the wood for floors, beams, doors, windows and, more rarely, lintels for doorways instead of the more usual stone – were all taken from the surrounding terrain. Unsurprisingly, although the general appearance of the rural villages and towns of Umbria hardly changes from one side of the region to the other, their individual characteristics do.

The shape, colour and quality of things like bricks and roof tiles, all of which were hand-made, vary from valley to valley. In the past,

This Renaissance marble portal is in sharp contrast to the stone and brick wall, half hidden beneath the stucco, that surrounds it. Two great doors, pierced by smaller ones for easier access, open to an inner courtyard.

Often incorporated into the buildings of Amelia are fragments dating from the Roman period and even earlier. This inscribed marble slab is now part of one of the town's gates. It adds stability to the rough wall of Roman cut stone, terracotta bricks and rubble.

LEFT: ON THE DEFENSIVE

Now abandoned, Postignano, near Sellano in northern Umbria, survives almost intact in its medieval state. Each stone-built tower is a private fortress into which the inhabitants could retreat in times of danger. Even the windows, small and watchful, seem determined to exclude as much light as possible.

LEFT: THE GREEN HEART OF ITALY

Umbria, where St Francis once perceived most acutely the hand of his Creator, is best observed from the ramparts of its remote medieval hill towns. Little has changed in these ancient centres, each one once a 'bedroom' community for the contadini *(peasant tenant farmers) who worked in the fields during the day.*

RIGHT: ST FRANCIS OF ASSISI
The remains of this medieval ogee-arched window, long bricked up, have been used to house a ceramic picture of Umbria's best-known saint.

RIGHT: CHURCH FORTRESS
Skirting the base of this hill-top church and campanile, the village houses — their façades cliff-like — offer protection as though they were the bastions of a castle.

when the valleys were inaccessible, each one would have had its own tiny furnace capable of making no more than about 1,000–1,200 bricks and 300 roof tiles at a time. While basic techniques of production did not vary much from place to place, the finish was very individual and often fairly eccentric. The brickmaker (*spiantore*) would have pressed wooden frames, a rectangular one for regular bricks, a trapezoidal one for vault bricks, into a layer of gluey clay, levelling off the surface with his fingers. The marks he left behind him, now hidden in the depths of the wall, are possibly his only memorial. Easier to see are the marks he left on the roof tiles: before he lifted the flat trapezoidal plate of clay cut in the shape of a tile, he levelled it, again with his fingers, then slapped in on to a curved wooden mould which was whipped out from beneath it before the clay dried on to it. Out in the sun where the tile lay for four to five days, his fingermarks dried where he had left their imprints. They give each tile its characteristic striated top.

There are other variations from area to area: at the northern end of the Tiber Valley, beyond Città di Castello, where the Apennines touch the remote hilly extremity of Umbria, the walls of the lone rural houses

LEFT: A *CASA COLONICA* FORTIFIED
This rural farmhouse developed around the base of a medieval watchtower. Stone-built to withstand attack from marauding armies, it has been in use for over half a millennium and is still as good as new.

are made of sandstone which is used practically as it emerges from the ground. Regularly shaped blocks and flat stones are laid together using a dry construction technique, also well suited to roofs and pavements.

Not far away in the Umbertide district, south of Città di Castello, rows of limestone blocks are used, giving the wall a far more regular appearance. Any gaps in between were filled with splinters of stone and brick of different colour. The profiles of these buildings are rough and ready, though the door and window surrounds are normally more formal, made from large, crisply cut blocks of stone adding a degree of support to the surrounding wall. By contrast, at Gubbio in the north-east, the steely-grey granite from which most of the buildings are made is crisp, angular and dark, exaggerating the town's martial appearance. This is at odds with the dusty, sun-baked character of the burnished gold stone of places like Assisi and Todi.

Often in Umbria the advantages of a particular site were recognized by subsequent generations and it was therefore occupied without a break: by 'reading' the masonry and the variations in construction and repair, it is possible to trace the various epochs of a house's history. If the plaster surface were stripped right back, you might see the blockwork repairs of the Middle Ages making good a collapsing brick wall built by the Romans; terracotta Roman tiles wedged into an old opening, filling a gap, in the medieval masonry; medieval window arches, some Gothic, others rounded as the fashion changed, each one a neat juxtaposition of precisely carved blocks, but blocked up as the building expanded and needs changed; a delicately carved Renaissance window might have been put into an older wall in search of a symmetry that never concerned builders a century earlier; a humble towerhouse in the thirteenth century, built on to the stump of a Roman building, might have become a provincial palazzo in the fifteenth.

All over rural Umbria, the beauty of the buildings and their relationship with their surroundings depend on a careful balance between formal and informal elements: between the houses and the surrounding fields; between the profile of medieval town and the contour of a hill. Age-old poverty and relative inaccessibility have helped preserve this balance, and it is the most endearing characteristic of the region today.

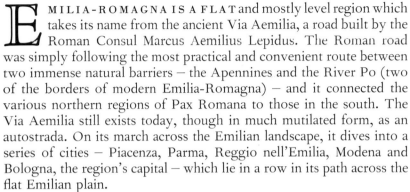

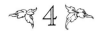

EMILIA-ROMAGNA

MILIA-ROMAGNA IS A FLAT and mostly level region which takes its name from the ancient Via Aemilia, a road built by the Roman Consul Marcus Aemilius Lepidus. The Roman road was simply following the most practical and convenient route between two immense natural barriers – the Apennines and the River Po (two of the borders of modern Emilia-Romagna) – and it connected the various northern regions of Pax Romana to those in the south. The Via Aemilia still exists today, though in much mutilated form, as an autostrada. On its march across the Emilian landscape, it dives into a series of cities – Piacenza, Parma, Reggio nell'Emilia, Modena and Bologna, the region's capital – which lie in a row in its path across the flat Emilian plain.

Immediately to the north of the Via Aemilia this plain extends towards the south bank of the Po which runs along Emilia-Romagna's northern frontier with the Veneto. To the south it creeps slowly towards the foothills of the Apennines, gradually melting into them to form an impenetrable barrier between Emilia-Romagna and Tuscany which lies beyond.

Flat plain and rugged mountainous valleys could not be more at odds with one another. They cradle the two faces of Emilia-Romagna, the one rich, fertile and burgeoning with life; the other rather ugly, bare and desolate. The feeling of loneliness up in the Apennines is exaggerated by an acute contrast with the frenetic activity of life on the *pianura*, the plain. Here there are towns and villages, farms, avenues of dead-straight poplars and cypresses lining roads and property boundaries, and rows of fruit trees criss-crossing the patchwork pattern of fields for as far as the eye can see.

The flats of Emilia-Romagna mutate into a variety of different forms along the Adriatic coast and inland in and around the Po Delta, as far as Ferrara. Wide, sandy beaches fringe the land's junction with the sea, while just a little way inland the country is riddled with a series of interlocking lagoons, waterways, canals and reedy

LEFT: BY THE BORDER
The influence of the Veneto, just a few kilometres away, is clearly visible here. This building could almost be a country villa like those on the banks of the Brenta Canal near Treviso. It is, in fact, a farmhouse, albeit a patrician one.

LEFT: TORRE DELL'ABATE, MESOLA
Outside Mesola is the seventeenth-century Torre dell'Abate, which operates the hydraulics of the local system of canals. Built of fine, small bricks with some very elegant detailing, particularly at cornice level, it also acted as a bridge and defensive lookout.

marshes. This waterlogged landscape, particularly around Ferrara and Ravenna, has its own peculiar character and distinctive architectural vernacular.

The flavour of the latter is often very idiosyncratic: for example, in the Ferrarese district, and around the little town of Comacchio which, like Venice, is built on a series of canals, there are a handful of buildings spanning the odd canal which are part watchtower and part bridge. Built from the seventeenth century, their primary function was to contain the hydraulics of the adjacent locks, canals and waterways and the workings of the system of drainage for the surrounding fields. But they also doubled as a tollgate for travellers over the waterway and as a watchtower in defence of the surrounding district.

One of these, the Torre dell' Abate near Mesola, sits on a series of low-slung arches which march through a waterway from one bank to the other. At ground level is the roadway which, crossing the water, burrows like a tunnel through the building. Flanking it, and still on the 'bridge' portion of the structure, are rooms which contained the machinery for the lock system. A barrel-vaulted ceiling holds up the three-bayed building above while on the very top there is a small, almost square, tower-like room a single bay wide. This served as the lookout post.

Like most buildings in Emilia-Romagna, it was built entirely of brick – even the cornices were fashioned from bricks protruding from the wall surface – and there is a terracotta pantiled roof. There are interesting variations on the design of this type of building: some were built beside the waterway and not over it. There are plenty of nineteenth-century ones, like the Impianto Idraulico Randola, also near Mesola, which have a neo-classical feel about them. In this particular one the wall surface is articulated by flat, shallow pilasters (rectangular columns which project only slightly from a wall) and the edges of the building are marked by heavy quoins.

The countryside around the Po Delta also contains one other type of building which is undoubtedly the result of years of adapting to the constantly changing patterns of this landscape and of trial-and-error building practice: fishermen's cottages-cum-storage cabins made of brick and built wherever the land was firm or on whatever had been

BELOW: AIRING THE PIGSTY
Bologna, the capital of Emilia, is often known as La Rossa *('The Red') because of the colour of its brickwork. Even the lowliest pigsty in the flat Emilian landscape is a fiery red. This pigsty is aired by means of a triangular opening lined with header bricks, creating a simple but satisfying pattern.*

LEFT: COMACCHIO

The proximity of the Veneto is reflected here at Comacchio, a town riven by a series of canal-like waterways. The 'two-up, two-down' dwellings, the fishing smacks drawn up outside them, are fishermen's houses.

reclaimed from the water. Generally long, thin, rectangular buildings devoid of any ornament whatever, they hug the banks on the very edge of the water.

At one time they were accompanied by long thin buildings constructed using a wooden skeleton or frame which was driven into the mud then clad in reeds. This building, a boathouse-workshop, would have jutted out into the water, and was entered by boat via a large square opening cut into the reed wall. At the other end there was a door to terra firma. The design of these boathouses varied considerably: sometimes a simple 'A'-frame building rather like a tent was all that was required; elsewhere it was a substantial rectangular structure with a hipped roof looking rather like an English tithe barn.

If the land was not as firm as it might have been or, equally, if the resident fishermen were extremely poor, the accompanying house might also be made of wood and reeds (the Po Delta then, as now, was thick with them). A very simple, and most probably very damp, dwelling was attached to a brick chimney whose smoking outlet soared way up above the thatched mesh of the roof below for the sake of safety. Life here was very basic: water and fish were taken from the canal and reeds cut for the fire. And until fifty years ago nothing much had changed.

Styles of buildings in all classes vary from one end of Emilia-Romagna to the other. In the fifteenth and the sixteenth centuries buildings in the orbit of, say, Bologna were not quite the same as those in the Ferrarese (the countryside around Ferrara). These two cities, thriving artistic centres at the time, developed their own styles based on Renaissance forms emanating from contemporary Florence. Each then became an important starting point for further developments throughout their respective areas, and even today the architecture of Bologna is not quite the same as that of the Ferrarese.

However, both these cities, along with the rest of Emilia-Romagna, possess an ancient tradition of building in brick – *a cotto*. Since Roman times the use of brick has been very widespread indeed and is possibly the most common feature of the buildings of this region. The use of brick affected the character and style of the buildings, except, of course, where the use of stone required other forms.

RIGHT: BRICK AND STUCCO

The church led the way by decreeing that its buildings should be plastered over in deep red stucco. Nowadays, thanks to the presence of clay, selenite and sandstone in Emilia-Romagna, stucco in warm, brick-red, ochre-yellow and beige is one of the most characteristic features of the province's buildings.

RIGHT: BRICK ON BRICK

Intricate exposed brickwork is characteristic of Emilian towns and villages: architects eschewed marble and ornate stucco for honest red fired bricks made locally. The use of these ancient cotti, *known even to the Romans, developed into a highly refined art form: they were used to make moulding columns, capitals and entablatures.*

A natural outcome of this widespread use of brick was the incorporation of terracotta ornament as an accompaniment to the brickwork. This too has a long tradition in Emilia-Romagna and is more highly refined in urban areas than in rural ones. In Ferrara and surrounding districts, for example, the terracotta ornament to the brickwork is often characterized by quite fantastical applications of small-scale vegetal elements, garlands and swags.

On the poorer houses decoration was simply limited to what could be done with the brick itself: a heavily rusticated brick cornice steps up to and nestles under the eaves, topped by the undulating edge of a pantiled roof. There might also be a stringcourse of a single line of bricks protruding from the façade between the ground and first floors and between the first and second.

BELOW: VERSATILITY IN TERRACOTTA
*Terracotta window surrounds and sills
are just another variation on the
terracotta theme. Here simple
mouldings are both finely moulded
and elegant.*

Clay, selenite and sandstone, in rich, earth colours, were the typical materials found in much of the region, an area which is crossed by a chalk vein stretching from Yugoslavia to France. From these the raw brick of the Emilian buildings derives its colour. And if the brick of the façades was not exposed then it was rendered in stucco which was washed over in deep, hot, earthy colours – red, terracotta, turmeric, ochre, rust – pigments which also derived their hues from the local terrain. On a hot summer's day this alone seems to increase the intensity of the heat beating down on the buildings, thus encouraging the use of one of Emilia-Romagna's other universal characteristics – arcaded porticoes. Another feature peculiar to Emilia-Romagna is the shape and the look of the rural farmhouses, the *case coloniche*. These two features alone would undoubtedly indicate to the perceptive traveller his regional whereabouts.

Porticoes line the streets and encircle the squares, sheltering pedestrians from inclement weather of winter and summer in towns and villages all over the region. In the Middle Ages, as the population expanded within the confines of walled cities and towns, the *Comune*, the local council, racking their brains to come up with an easy solution to an acute housing shortage, hit upon the idea of building on to the façades of the buildings already lining the streets. This narrowed the streets considerably but a walkway was left beneath each extension so that the wooden floors of the latter were the ceilings of the porticoed walkways beneath them. This solution was particularly pertinent in Bologna which from the eleventh century suffered more problems than most cities because of the influx of students seeking accommodation at its newly opened university. In the rural towns and villages – as at Cento between Ferrara and Modena, for example – the porticoes served a practical purpose, providing protection from the sun and from the rain, and encouraging social contact out in the street.

Porticoes eventually became compulsory adjuncts, the minimum height being the easy transit of a man on horseback. Only the very grandest palaces infringed the law: creating a link with the plebeian passers-by was considered by the most aristocratic in the towns to be way beneath them so they snootily omitted porticoes from their building programmes.

BELOW: OLD AND NEW
*New does not necessarily mean
twentieth century in Italy; it might
simply mean 'less old'. Here a 'new'
wall is opened up to reveal ancient
beams still in situ. Below, wooden
posts and beams form the construction
of an arcaded pavement.*

LEFT: HOT TERRACOTTA
*The most common building material in
Emilia-Romagna is brick. Here the
pointed-arched windows have
terracotta and brick mouldings at their
edges, while the arcades and the
porticoes lining the streets are covered
by brick vaults and held up by brick
piers and columns.*

RIGHT: WEATHER-PROOFED
SPACE SAVERS
Vaults, arcades and covered outside places are a feature of all Emilian towns and villages.

ABOVE: BRICK AND MARBLE
Glass fills what was once a void on either side of the central marble column of this little window. Now reflecting the buildings opposite, it once opened onto an internal gallery.

RIGHT: FERRARA: CASTELLO ESTENSE
In the middle of Ferrara, the vast Castello Estense hogs the limelight while simple but elegant buildings adjacent to it remain unnoticed. What a pity: here simple devices like segmental or triangular pediments alternate above the windows, adding subtle variety to an otherwise bland façade.

In the Middle Ages the porticoes were supported by wooden columns. Later, in the fourteenth and fifteenth centuries, they were held up by graceful, slender stone or brick arches and deftly finished with carved capitals and other decoration. Every portico has its own history and lore, as can be seen from the individual friezes, capitals, heraldic and ancestral coats of arms, and anthropomorphic, floral and sacred decoration.

The second most characteristic feature of the Emilian landscape, the red-brick *casa colonica*, is quite different in form from its counterparts in Umbria and Tuscany. The Emilian farmhouse is often a substantial building which, in the half-light, could easily be mistaken for a large country seat. In some cases, particularly with the larger houses, the brick walls might be articulated elegantly but simply with shallow 'blind' arcading (arches applied to the wall surface as decoration) detailed with simplified capitals and approached, or at least surrounded, by a row of poplars or cypresses. However, such bulk often means that the building is multi-purpose and incorporates the house as well as the barn, stables and hayloft, under a single pitched roof.

RIGHT: DECORATING WITH BRICK
Who needs stucco or even sculpture when you can use brick and local clay as ornament? Articulation of the wall surface is provided by recessed and advancing plains of brick. The storage space is aerated by removing individual bricks to form a geometric pattern of holes.

RIGHT: CATHEDRALS IN
THE COUNTRYSIDE
The relationship of this Emilian barn to the neighbouring farmhouse illustrates its importance. The barn is vast — the cathedral of the countryside — while the house is almost insignificant in comparison.

The house has regular rows of sometimes shuttered windows while the barn is reached through a single arch or pair of arches running from the ground right up to the eaves. This is by far the most interesting — and magnificent — building in an Emilian farmyard, and it is subject to a number of variations in layout and construction. In some cases there is a massive brick structure (brick walls and floor) just beyond the arched opening which contains the stables at ground level and the hayloft above. The brick vaults of the stables (among the most intricately constructed pieces of architecture found anywhere in the Emilia-Romagna) form the floor of the hayloft above it, the latter becoming a sort of gallery which is reached by a ladder (with the hay winched into it via a large hook and pulley suspended nearby). The hayloft does not have its own roof but shares an open-trussed one with the rest of the barn. This strange building-within-a-building arrangement does have its advantages: if the barn itself happens to be open on all four sides, then at least the livestock and hay can be kept secure and dry within it; having the two share a roof is just a matter of economical

LEFT: RURAL DIGNITY
Simple shapes and harmonious proportions – a row of perfect blind arches pierced at regular intervals by shallow pilasters – give this building its dignity.

LEFT: HOUSE AND BARN
In some cases the house and the barn are part of the same structure, the former playing second fiddle to the latter. While the house is virtually devoid of architectural adornment, to the point at which it might be described as nondescript, the barn is filled with 'incident' – an opening with a stair, varied construction materials, and changes in scale.

planning. In addition to this stable-hayloft building-within-a-building, there might also be a series of brick piers or an intricate web of wooden staves holding up the rest of the barn roof.

On other occasions the barn is quite separate from the stables and hay store, yet contained under the same roof structure, each unit divided from the next by a wall, and each entered through individual openings. Sometimes a single block of buildings contains house and barn as well as stables and hayloft. The central unit – the barn – has the biggest entrance, say, a series of huge arched doors. The stables and hayloft are to the left of this and the house to the right. The three areas share a common roof.

In other cases the barn and house are in quite separate buildings but within a formal relationship to each other. They might be at right angles to one another or facing each other across a brick-paved

LEFT: ROUGH RUSTICITY

The casa colonica *of the Apennines is quite different in appearance from that of the great Emilian plain. While the barn is all-important in the latter, an illustration of the fecundity and profitability of the land, in the Appenines it is the house that matters. Here a dovecot rises above this farmhouse.*

LEFT: OCHRE AND TERRACOTTA

The buildings of Emilia-Romagna are, almost universally, a hot, dusty colour, the colour of the ochre clay of the region. Pantiles, building bricks (stone is used only rarely), even the wash on the stucco where it is used to cover the brick, are terracotta-coloured. Here banks of orange roofs cap the town buildings, the pantiles a shape used since time immemorial.

courtyard, each with a pitched roof, their bulk similar in mass and in shape. And characteristically, the astonishing thing about these rural structures is the excellence of their proportions which, for all their simplicity, gives them an aloof dignity of their own.

This dwelling of the share-cropping tenant or labourer is quite unlike the country villa or seat of the local landowner, however modest the latter might be. The latter would undoubtedly have certain characteristics which 'ennoble' it, setting it apart from its humbler neighbour. While it might have the same surface articulation – the blind arcading and the stepped brick cornice already mentioned – it will almost certainly have a raised floor, a *piano nobile*, approached from the drive or entrance courtyard via a short flight of formal, ceremonial steps. According to the sixteenth-century Venetian architect Andrea Palladio, this arrangement was to prevent the master from being disturbed by the outdoor work, or interfering in it himself. Above it, under the eaves, is an attic storey; below it on the ground floor, kitchens and cellars. This arrangement is quite alien to the farmhouses of the region where the farmers and labourers enter at ground level straight into the kitchen, the other rooms being spread about between two or even three other storeys. At the top of the steps a pedimented entrance door in a stuccoed façade might be flanked by a series of tall windows placed symmetrically on either side of it, aligned with small windows in the attic storey and at the ground-floor level.

The same sense of rhythm is quite common in even the roughest *casa colonica*. In a house of, say, seven bays, every alternate opening in the wall might be a door. There might be two windows between every door, the gaps between door and window far larger than that between the two windows. The variations are endless and, stumbled upon in some remote, rural enclave, delightful to discover.

The designs of the country buildings of Emilia-Romagna give great dignity to a rough-and-ready rural life. They provide it with a sense of *gravitas* which it would not otherwise have had. This, married to the huge scale of some of the farms which were built on the proceeds of a hugely fertile region, means that often the rural buildings of Emilia-Romagna are, perversely, amongst the grandest buildings to be found anywhere in Italy.

RIGHT: DECAYING GRANDEUR
The ramshackle former seat of a country landowner, this building now contains lowly barns and storerooms, even cattle. Evidence of its former grandeur can be seen in the tower marking each of its four corners.

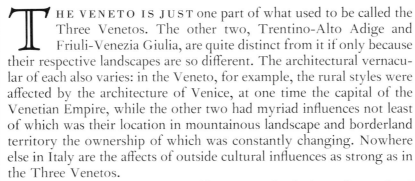

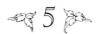

THE VENETO

T HE VENETO IS JUST one part of what used to be called the Three Venetos. The other two, Trentino-Alto Adige and Friuli-Venezia Giulia, are quite distinct from it if only because their respective landscapes are so different. The architectural vernacular of each also varies: in the Veneto, for example, the rural styles were affected by the architecture of Venice, at one time the capital of the Venetian Empire, while the other two had myriad influences not least of which was their location in mountainous landscape and borderland territory the ownership of which was constantly changing. Nowhere else in Italy are the affects of outside cultural influences as strong as in the Three Venetos.

Two-thirds of the Veneto itself consists of a fairly well-populated flat plain called the *pianura padana*, which is made up of a network of interminable flat fields with bluish mountains on the horizon. Shelley called it 'the green sea. . .the waveless plain. . .'. It is broken up by roads and railways, some fringed with dead-straight rows of trees, others with canals, between little brick towns and villages. This plain, often swathed in a thick impenetrable mist, stretches west to the shore of Lake Garda, south to the northern banks of the River Po and in the south-west near Padua spreads out around the Euganean Hills so that the latter – something of a geological oddity – seem to rise up like an island. Further north, beyond Asolo, it becomes hilly, reaching a dramatic climax amongst the jagged peaks of the Dolomites not far from Italy's border with Austria. Pockets of this dramatic landscape are very beautiful: around Asolo, for example, the Colli Asolani (the Asolo Hills) are small and hump-like, their crests fringed with cypresses. Here and there the occasional silhouette of a castle introduces a sharper line. These *colli* are a foretaste, in miniature, of the Alpine foothills around Monte Grappa not far away.

The Veneto is so influenced by Venice that it is easy to forget what lies beyond the watery confines of this famous city. Historically its tentacles have always reached out into the surrounding countryside in

LEFT: BASSANO

All over Bassano, buildings sport the characteristics of Venetian architecture – not surprisingly, as it happens, since this little town was a dependency of Venice for about 400 years of its life. At the same time, it also has many arcaded streets which are, of course, common throughout neighbouring Emilia-Romagna.

BELOW: WROUGHT IN IRON AND
PAINTED IN FRESCO
*An early eighteenth-century wrought-
iron balcony, in a vaguely Art
Nouveau style, is the perfect foil for the
faded fresco of sunflowers and leaves.*

an effort to dominate it. There is evidence of its presence in the architecture of towns, villages and rural enclaves all over the region. For example, it is quite common to find country town halls and important houses built in the Venetian Gothic style, with ogee-arched windows, even in quite small villages. And there are *piazze* up and down the region whose centres are watched over by a statue of the lion of St Mark, the symbol of the patron saint of Venice, perched on top of a column.

The Serene Republic of Venice – 'La Serenissima' as it was known – amassed its power during the Crusades in the eleventh, twelfth and thirteenth centuries when it was called upon to transport Christian armies to the East. Quick to spot the lucrative trading potential of this traffic with the Arab and the Byzantine civilizations and with Eastern Europe, the wily merchants of Venice were soon bringing back cloth, spices, coffee, gems, strange fruits and vegetables and slaves – Persians, Africans, Slavs. And, not surprisingly, the wealth of the republic multiplied on a grand scale until it became one of the richest states of the contemporary world.

On the back of all this exotic interchange, cultural influences drifted backwards and forwards from the eastern Mediterranean to Venice. Not least amongst these were foreign architectural styles, detailing and methods of craftsmanship. Perhaps St Mark's Cathedral in Venice, begun in 1063, is the most obvious example of the results of this traffic. Its magnificent lustre was created by architects who were most probably Byzantine and consequently way out of touch with what was going on in the rest of Italy. The use of costly materials, the lavish adornments of coloured marble and the accumulation of decorative ornament with a wealth of forms and motifs derives from this source.

Even the façades of the palaces in Venice's Grand Canal are a version of St Mark's Oriental splendour and its sense of display. There are tall, funnel-shaped chimneys, often ornately decorated; pointed and ogee-arched windows framed into rectangular panels; central loggias and balconies on the main façades; regularly spaced window openings and decorative patterns of openings in the wall, each one generally framed by lavish marble decoration.

RIGHT: IN THE CLUTCH OF
THE VENETIANS
*Throughout the Veneto even the
smallest town houses have been touched
by the influence of the architectural
style of Venice. Here windows are
fashioned in the Venetian Gothic
manner while the marble entrance
portal, with its florid adornments and
classical structure, is closer to the late
fifteenth century.*

RIGHT: SOMETHING OLD,
SOMETHING NEW

*The façade of this old building in the
centre of Conegliano is adorned with
delicate terracotta panels. Lower down,
stone-carved acanthus leaves – a
classical motif widely used in the
Renaissance – are carved out on every
stone of the arch.*

RIGHT: OUTSIDE INFLUENCES

*The mark of Venice, as before, is
displayed to great effect on the left-
hand building. To the right, a simpler,
almost Tuscan style of decoration
marks another influence.*

By the fifteenth century a remarkably rich and very distinctive regional style had emerged. This can be seen throughout the Veneto in the towns and rural villages under Venetian supremacy. While the grandest homes in Venice itself were adorned with real cut stone, marble panels and carvings, the homes of the local barons and dignitaries in these small towns and villages were stuccoed and then painted a *trompe l'oeil*. Although the window surrounds themselves might be cut from stone in ogee or pointed arch shapes, the various storeys are separated from one another by painted stringcourses and varying styles of 'stonework'. The ground-floor level might have painted rustication (simulating heavy, roughly dressed stonework intended to give the building a sense of brute strength at street level). There might be simulated carving in *grisaille* (painting executed in monochrome in shades of grey) between the upper windows – and possibly even whole scenes frescoed on to the wall, as at Feltre, gradually becoming lighter and more ornate towards the roof. There might even be areas of *sgrafitto*, decoration on plaster of incised patterns, the top coat being cut through to show a differently coloured

LEFT: FOLLINA

Discreetly Venetian, the houses of Follina mark the social standing of their occupants. There is a certain patrician respectability about the house in the background with its little balconies and their stone balustrades.

LEFT: VITTORIO VENETO

The farmhouse at Vittorio Veneto could almost be a palace on one of Venice's canals. Its façade is highly decorated with arches, hefty columns, two loggias, a heavy cornice and the two heraldic beasts, while the back and flanks of the building are anything but architectural showpieces.

LEFT: ASOLO'S CHIMNEYS
One of the most characteristic features of the architecture of this part of the Veneto are its chimneys – tall and usually decorated with a cap of terracotta pantiles and bricks. Each one is different, having simply evolved as the building work progressed.

coat beneath. Deep overhanging eaves are there to provide a modicum of protection from rain and snow.

The word 'rural' in parts of the Veneto has a strange ring to it. Instead of farmsteads locked in the midst of ploughed fields or lone hamlets buried deep within the folds of the hills, there are lone houses and small settlements on the edge of the Venetian lagoons, on islets separated by canals in flat, marshy and low-lying terrain. It seems rather surprising that this terrain can bear the weight of a building, let alone a whole village, but a little way beneath the sand and the mud there are thick layers of solid clay. The industrious inhabitants of early Venice made their foundations from thousands of wooden staves and piles; the Rialto Bridge in Venice, for example, a relatively small construction, made use of about 30,000 trees to give it solidity. For a bigger building or a whole village, hundreds of thousands of trees were required. In the very early days wood came from the *lidi*, the sandy frontiers between the lagoons and the sea which were covered with trees. Later, logs were floated down to the lagoons via rivers from the wooded Alpine valleys or brought to the region by sea from Dalmatia.

Venice might be the largest settlement in this strange topography but it is by no means the only significant one. Chioggia is one, Pellestrina, Torcello, Burano and Murano are others. All had close links with Venice over a period of centuries. Murano, for example, a small fishing village situated on the landward shore of its own lagoon about 80 kilometres (50 miles) north-east of Venice, was a small, introverted island village. Like other villages in the vicinity, even the simplest, poorest houses and cottages were distinctly Venetian in character with prominent and characteristic chimneys. All were – and still are – built of brick, with the occasional use of stone for details and in specific areas such as the door or window surrounds (head and sill only). Only rarely was stone used for the entire building.

One exception to this rule is the little village of Grado in the north, not far from the ruins of the Roman city of Aquileia. The proximity of this vast 'quarry' meant that even today the houses of Grado are built of stone rather than brick. Not only were the ruins very convenient, but re-used stone did not require the furnaces (and regular supplies of

BELOW: THE ULTIMATE ARTIFICE
Here, for all to see, the wear and tear and general neglect reveal the true face of the buildings of the Veneto – brick rendered in washed stucco. A simple balustrade of wood makes up the balcony, while deep openings above lead to the storage attics.

LEFT: VILLAGE SIMPLICITY

The village church and the simple village houses have their own charm: chimneys, regimented windows and banks of glowing orange terracotta pantiles. Even the treads of the steps have their own simple decoration — smooth round pebbles embedded mosaic-like into clay.

LEFT: OF STONE AND BRICK

Large stone quoins, the dressed stones at the corners of buildings, bring the eye to the turn of a wall. Visually and physically they complete the structure, giving it greater solidity. The windows on each floor are surrounded by bricks; the lower windows on the main floor, being bigger than those above, reflect the relative importance of the rooms within.

timber for their firing) that were needed to build towns of brick. Grado was also the last stronghold of the Venetian Empire. So while some of its houses' details are recognizably Venetian, they are mixed with elements that crept in from the territories of the neighbouring Habsburg Empire and the adjacent Islamic states of the Balkans.

Common to all the little villages in these wet, isolated parts are the small two-storeyed homes generally joined together in a terrace. Originally only one or two rooms big, they had to house families of up to six or eight people; families of fishermen, chandlers, boatbuilders and, originally, market gardeners who worked the flatlands beyond the villages. They are simple brick boxes with a tiled roof and prominent chimney devoid of all architectural pretensions (though nowadays, in places like Burano and Murano, the houses are painted in bright, attractive colours — blue, ochre, yellow, pink). Others, also built in simple terraces (*casette a schiera*), were slightly bigger with, on the ground floor, portico and shops from which a staircase led into the upper living rooms. This is a typically Venetian variant, much watered down, of a very old Roman arrangement. Even the homes of their

RIGHT: LIGHT, TEXTURE AND PATTERN
The charm of so many Italian buildings lies in the play of light across even plain washed surfaces, and in the tension between shapes of parts of a building and the patterns on them. Even the arch of a window and the semi-circular shape of a protruding balcony echo each other, though the shapes lie in different planes.

RIGHT: RICH AND POOR
Ionic pilasters, with acanthus-decorated capitals, flank the tall windows of the aristocratic mansion on the left. Lesser mortals make do with an enriched cornice, just below the eaves. Stone — a more expensive building material — is prominently displayed on the one, brick and plaster on the other.

wealthier neighbours who lived in small *palazzi* of, say, ten rooms, adhered to an ancient scheme which divided the façade of the building into three parts: a ground-floor entrance with, if the building was on the canal, a portico on the waterside; a central first-floor reception room; and then other chambers dispersed about the remaining storey. These patrician houses, occupying perhaps a significant spot in the main *piazza* or on the edge of the central *rio*, the narrow canal between the islets, showed much awareness of current fashion and style: they might be Gothic or Renaissance in detailing.

The *case padronali*, belonging to wealthy patrician landowners who lived in the city, can be found on the outskirts of the village or town and originally would have been either a summer retreat, a hunting lodge or a place where a mistress could be entertained in seclusion. Many survive, restored, and are a rather idiosyncratic 'find', a sort of urban palace building out in the 'wilds'.

In the *valle*, the shallow basins of enclosed water on the edge of the lagoons, are the isolated *casoni*, the houses or huts used by hunters and fishermen. In the past those belonging to noble Venetian families were

LEFT: SHOWPIECE
This folly-like and very pretentious piece of architecture may have begun life in the nineteenth century as a dovecot or a rural watchtower, though the external stucco is so well kept that its true age is masked. The approach façade receives all the attention: even the moulded stringcourses simply stop after they turn the corner.

LEFT: *CASA COLONICA*
Anything but pretentious, this house presents itself to the world for what it is: a rough, rural dwelling. It fulfils very well the function for which it was built, with small windows to keep out the hot summer sun and cold winter winds.

LEFT: FARMING ON THE GRAND SCALE
This house, now derelict, was the home of a patrician farmer who might have divided his time between town and country. Echoes of Palladio, a sixteenth-century architect and one of Italy's greatest and most influential, can be seen in the way the central block is flanked by two smaller wings. The tower, on the other hand, is a remnant of the distant past, when the house was a simple rural dwelling.

LEFT: PERFECTLY HUMBLE
Brushwood, firewood, crops and stores are protected from the rain by the deep overhanging eaves of this barn. The harmonious proportions of the building – the central doorway, the two perfectly framed flanking windows, the central pier above the door holding up the roof – point to an innate sense of design in even the most humble of builders.

quite grand with elaborate brick landing stages, stucco finishes to the façades and tall chimneys. The poorer versions, used not for sport but as a means of making a living, were made of timber, straw and reeds – probably not unlike the dwellings used by the earliest inhabitants of this region. Some still survive as workshops here and there, the fishing nets hung up to dry; these sheds are often more precious than people's homes because they are an essential part of their livelihoods.

In the fifteenth century there emerged in all regions of Italy a new type of building, namely the Renaissance villa. In the Veneto a whole series of formal elements of Venetian palace architecture provided some of the inspiration for this type. One such element was the antique Byzantine type of house, with an open porch and end projections with roofs ending in gables, which had become a characteristic of Venetian architecture. There is a theory that this was the progenitor of villa architecture throughout Italy.

Around Venice and as far afield as Vicenza can be found the villas of Andrea Palladio, perhaps the most important architect working in the sixteenth century in northern Italy. His villas – basically rectangular

RIGHT: THE TEMPLE FRONT

Out in the fields, this rural manor house on the banks of the Brenta canal, with its strict sense of symmetry, derives from the designs of the great Venetian architect, Palladio. Each part of the building relates to its neighbour in a strict rule of proportion.

RIGHT: MULTIPARTE, NEAR MASER

This villa is dominated by its central bay which receives nearly all the decoration, whether stone-carved balusters or simply deeply and finely cut stone.

blocks connected to subsidiary wings by straight or curving colonnades – spawned a whole range of lesser rural homes. A strict sense of symmetry about a central axis was all-important and each part of the building was related to its neighbouring part by a strict rule of proportion. Curiously abstract, Palladio's buildings are devoid of external decoration; even the windows, simple rectangular openings in the wall, are very often unadorned by pediments or architrave. Many of his works tend towards smooth surfaces, right angles and plain cubic forms.

The Palladian style became an almost universal villa type out in the countryside away from the city. It was mimicked throughout the *pianura padana* and right up as far as Bassano del Grappa and Conegliano, enjoying great popularity when, as the Turkish advance in the eastern Mediterranean and the discovery of America sounded the death knell for Venetian overseas trade, the republic turned its attention to the development of its own countryside for farming. The vast swamps of the river valleys were drained and country estates became a lucrative source of income to the landed nobility.

BELOW: MOTHER OF GOD
Prominently displayed in a niche, a plaster statue of the Virgin. Rough-cast wall panels are preferred to stucco, and regular window surrounds provide a meet geometric setting for the niche.

These Venetian country seats were soon surrounded by fields and vineyards. Unlike their Florentine equivalents, the estates were agriculturally productive. As well as the villa, most included houses for farmworkers, barns, wine cellars, grain stores and stables. The aristocratic versions of the genre, with their *piano nobili*, their high basements and their great central pediment rising above the roof on the main axis, are easily recognizable.

Their lesser counterparts are just as charming with nearly as much distinction. The countryside here is so fertile that it is scarcely surprising that people could afford to build these gracious houses. Even the peasants lived in relative ease. Though many buildings mimic the grander villas in, for example, the way their windows are grouped and in their use of brick and wood faced with stucco, they are none the less very different even down to the lack of formality in their landscape surroundings. They were used for very different purposes: one for relaxation and social activities during the *villeggiatura* months, the other a year-round home, not of labourers or cowherds but of prosperous farmers.

Italian builders, in particular Venetian ones, seem to have had a passion for composition and continuity of design: a barn might be arranged on an axis with the front door of the house, the homes of the labourers laid out symmetrically on either side of it facing a small courtyard. Nothing is haphazard, nothing left to chance.

Whatever the scale of the buildings, whatever their use and whoever owned them, few ever really escape the clutches of the rich cultural legacy of Venice. Equally, few are imbued with the same faded sense of melancholy so prevalent in Venice itself. Here, amongst the fields, there is vitality; and for every country house that is abandoned – built by patrician families who have long since ceased to exist – there are quantities of other, lesser buildings still playing an active part in the daily life of the Veneto.

RIGHT: MAROSTICA
The large keystone (the central stone of an arch) and the arch itself provides a dramatic foreground through which to see this little street scene in Marostica. The arch links the undercroft storage area of the house to the street.

6

LOMBARDY
AND THE LAKES

L OMBARDY AND ITS NEAR neighbour Piedmont are two of
the most conspicuously prosperous regions in Italy. Here, in
the industrial heartland, great power and wealth have given the
locals the highest standard of living in the country. Efficient and
successful, the people of both regions have organized their territory
into a patchwork of prosperous factories and richly fertile fields and
farms, producing a variety of goods ranging from rice to silk to cars.

Situated between the Alps in the north and the River Po in the
south, Lombardy jostles for space with Piedmont, Emilia-Romagna,
the Veneto and Trentino-Alto Adige. Unsurprisingly, around its
edges the region takes on not only the topographical characteristics of
its neighbours but also their architectural styles.

As the northernmost province of Italy, Lombardy was more often
than not the main route used to enter the Italian peninsula. Its history
has been extremely turbulent and not infrequently punctuated by
violence. The Etruscans, Umbrians and Celts all enjoyed periods of
dominance in these parts, as did the Romans, who gave the region a
semblance of stability for the first time in its history, and the
Langobardi, the Germanic tribe which gave Lombardy its name and –
or so it is claimed – the Milanesi their above-average height. After the
reign of Charlemagne as Holy Roman Emperor, Lombardy was
subject to almost continuous feuding between powerful family
dynasties – the Viscontis, the Sforzas and the Gonzagas. Later
ownership of Lombardy was contested by the French, Spanish and
Austrians, all of whom at various times attempted to incorporate it
into their empires. Each of these left their mark.

The region was therefore subject to myriad artistic and architectural
influences from east, west, north and south. In Lombardy's Alpine
districts, for example, but for certain distinctive local characteristics,
the buildings might easily be in Switzerland or in France. Likewise the

LEFT: OVERLOOKING LAKE COMO
On the edge of Lake Como, this modest little town is a mixture of small, boxy private villas and apartment houses. Most are devoid of decoration but still unmistakeably Lombardian in tone, with their stucco decoration, wide eaves and great banks of terracotta roof tiles.

architecture of the Orobi Alps above Bergamo, still in Lombardy, is not so very different from that of the Dolomitic area around Bolzano in neighbouring Trentino. Neither for that matter is the architecture of the Lombardy plain (on either side of the River Po) so very different from that around Bologna in Emilia-Romagna.

There is never a dull moment in any trip across Lombardy – or Piedmont, for that matter. Geographically, Lombardy is probably as varied as any region you could possibly hope to find: flat in the south and south-east, mountainous in the north, hilly in the west. Here and there the landscape is pierced by lakes, some of which – Garda, Como and Maggiore – are so large that they seem more like inland seas. The lakes, with their plunging Alps, forests and waterfalls, are to Lombardy what the lagoons are to Venice. They relieve that feeling of being enclosed which might otherwise be stifling. Some of them, such as Lake Maggiore, have extreme varieties of scenery: lowlands in the south around the city of Varese, with the mountains rising higher and higher as you go northwards, and the scenery reverberating with increasing drama. Even Piedmont's character alters from north to south, from the Swiss–French Alps through the hills of the Langhe and Monferrato to the plain in the east which runs into Lombardy.

While Lombardy contains one of the largest flat areas in the whole of Italy – lying along the edge of the Po, a sluggish, yellowish river fed and fattened by the many tributaries from the Alps and the Apennines – it also encompasses almost every topographic variation that can be found in the rest of the country. From pleasant, rolling hillside to craggy, inaccessible gorge or valley; from high mountain to flat plain laced by canals which are fed by Alpine water all year round, the landscape of Lombardy is a rough and silent introduction to what to expect of the terrain of the Veneto, Emilia-Romagna, Trentino-Alto Adige and Liguria – even Tuscany and Umbria. Climb up to the roof of the Duomo in Milan, at the heart of Lombardy, and beyond the flat landscape around the city you will see the shadows of the Alps round Como on Lake Como only about 30 kilometres (18 miles) away.

There are many similarities in the architecture of Lombardy and Piedmont. Unsurprisingly, such variety affects the region's buildings and the types of materials available for their construction. From

RIGHT: MENAGGIO
Perched on the side of a mountain, high above Lake Como, this villa is designed to offer the best possible view of one of Italy's most beautiful lakes. The lookout tower and open belvedere of this nineteenth-century mansion provide an ideal viewing point.

Banks of modest peasant houses with pitched, terracotta pantiled roofs nestle together as they stagger up the mountainside. Although roofing materials vary only marginally in shape, size and design, individual roofs acquire texture and pattern with age.

Lombardy's lakesides to the high Alpine valley districts that touch Switzerland, there is a long-standing tradition of using heavy wood or heavy wood and stucco on a wide variety of buildings, from houses to barns and other associated farm and storage buildings. Although these structures use the same logs and slates found in the mountain architecture of France and Switzerland, they are far more open and their interiors are far more interesting spatially.

This openness most probably evolved from the fact that the Italian builders have as their northern barriers the highest mountains in Europe. Thus protected from cold northern blasts and responding to available sunshine, the locals build on to their structures balconies where they store – and dry – their corn, grain and other agricultural products, as well as their washing. The outside walls of these balconies is not some fancy wrought-iron screen but a lattice of wooden strutts which lets in air but keeps out the rain. It is not unusual, driving through some Alpine district in deepest winter when the buildings are laden with snow which blots out the landscape, to see washing drying in the sun.

Banks of modest peasant houses with pitched roofs nestle together as they stagger up the mountainsides. The bulk of each building is made of wood, while the ground floor and the cellars that reach deep into the hillside are built of stone, and the roof, heavy and protective, is covered in slate.

The basic form of these buildings is common to all of Alpine Lombardy. However, in north-eastern Lombardy, where the region touches the Dolomites of the Trentino-Alto Adige, the buildings have one distinctive characteristic which is a relic of a tradition once very common in Italy: their roofs are made of straw, not just a straightforward thatch, but a very decorative plaiding. This tradition, which can still be seen just beyond the northern tip of Lake Garda, probably survived because of the area's relative isolation. Its use probably derived from the low working buildings of the lagoonsides in the Veneto and its gradual disappearance is without doubt due to its vulnerability to hazards like fire.

In the rare instances where thatch is still found, it is most typically on a type of construction where the lower walls are of stone rendered

RIGHT: ALPINE MODESTY

In the more remote Alpine hill villages, outside balconies are used for storing firewood, corn, or even washing. A deep overhang of the roof above protects this area from snow and rain. The buildings are constructed from stone, brick, timber and slate, and have, in many instances, withstood the ravages of centuries of winter storms.

LEFT: ORTA SAN GIULIO
No other region of Italy is as varied as Lombardy with its lofty northern valleys, flat Po plain in the south, and undulating hills in between. The architecture reflects these variations: here the almost Germanic architecture of this village on the edge of Lake Orta indicates links with Austria or Switzerland, while the Mediterranean sunshine announces that this is, in fact, Italy.

LEFT: DISASTER INSURANCE
Medieval farm buildings, restored and cared for, sport religious frescoes intended to protect against disaster.

in smooth stucco and finished in whitewash and the upper ones are of timber. The ratio of stucco and whitewash to timber seems arbitrary at first; however, on closer inspection stone tends to be used for the outer walls of rooms commonly in use. The heat retention qualities of the materials are obvious, hence this arrangement. The attics, on the other hand, are made of wood and the roofing materials of local slate.

By contrast to Lombardy's mountain architecture, down on the flat banks of the River Po the buildings are long and low. They seem to hug the flat landscape. The smaller farms have stables and storage at one end and the house at the other, although the two may be joined as a long narrow unit generally facing south. Some are built around a courtyard. These are known as the *cascine*, and are generally medieval and built of brick (here known as *campone*). Some have a small tower containing a bell over the owner's house.

The architecture of the plain is hugely appealing for the simple logic of its geometry. There is a great sense of design here, an almost mathematical purity that is found nowhere else in Italy. It can be seen in the great square barns with their pyramidal roofs, in the fenestration of a farmhouse and its outbuildings, and in the relationship of the various parts to each other across the farmyard. The simple structural elements, like the piers, are shorn of decoration, but the way in which they are grouped is based on carefully calculated proportions and a keen sense of space.

The brick vaulted ceilings of barns and cellars are low and broad, the spaces beneath wide and airy. The effect is rather sober; possibly it derives from a synthesis of Tuscan and Lombard architectural traditions where one, with its emphasis on spatial proportions and architectural order, is united with the other's indigenous use of brickwork.

Brick is the most widely used building material in Lombardy. One result of this is the taste for large expanses of wall, the articulation of which tends to be done only in the shallowest relief and with a finely tuned sense of proportion.

In conjunction with brick, terracotta – particularly for ornament – is traditionally the other most prevalent characteristic of Lombardy's buildings, both rural and urban. In the north of Italy the first signs of the architecture of fifteenth-century Florence appeared in a riot of

RIGHT: ALTERNATIVE DECORATION
Religious imagery is a common sight all over Italy. In some cases its presence makes up, visually, for the distinct lack of architectural decoration elsewhere. Protected from the rain and the snow by the wide overhanging eaves, the only enemy is the sun.

RIGHT: SEASONAL RELIEF
A loggia running along the upper floor of a house has been filled in for use as an extra room. Once the arches along the front of it were open, providing the members of the household with space in which to work. In winter they would be protected from the rain, and in summer the shade provided welcome relief from the sun.

LEFT: ORNAMENTAL
VERSUS STRUCTURAL

*Stucco quoins, here at Cannobio, Lake
Maggiore, give not only character to
this façade, but visually they give it
force, even stability. Making them the
colour of stone rather than white-
washing them — as the wall surface
once was — re-inforces this artifice.
Their presence creates an interesting
visual tension between the ornamental
and the structural.*

LEFT: REAL AND FAKE
*In order to match the window on the
left, the window on the right is a
painted* trompe l'oeil. *In the eternal
search for symmetry — an habitual
preoccupation of Italian builders — the
owner of this building has prepared a
faithful copy of the real thing. So
perfected was the painter's technique
that at a glance the artifice is
barely noticeable.*

terracotta decoration that was Gothic in conception and method of application but Renaissance in form. The architectural adornments typical of the Renaissance period — mouldings and so forth — were treated as ornament, thus helping to define one of the most noteworthy characteristics of the buildings of the region: a taste for hearty, effervescent surface decoration, particularly on the façades of churches, palaces and civic buildings. The proximity of Venice and its exuberant architecture was an obvious influence, though where Venetian decoration articulates the wall surface, Lombard decoration simply sits on top of it.

As anywhere else, the architecture of Lombardy responded to its locale. An awareness of how to adapt a building in response to the sun is something builders were aware of long before the advent of the twentieth century and its electric blinds. For example, it is quite common in the north of Lombardy to find as many windows and other apertures as can be managed on the south façades of the houses, while the north walls, except for small ventilation openings, are blank against the wintry blasts beating down on them from the Alps.

LEFT: PATTERN AND MOVEMENT
The beauty of this wall lies in the delicate pattern of movement from the central arched window, matched symmetrically by a replica on either side, through the flanking shallow recessed panels to the series of deep circular openings above. Shadows cast by the differing depths of wall surface are as good as any pattern made by a craftsman.

LEFT: CUT DOWN TO SIZE
An ancient window in a Bellagio building, long defunct in its original purpose, is reused in the best possible way. Most probably the room onto which it casts light was partitioned and made smaller, thus calling for individual windows much reduced in scale.

LEFT: LAKESIDE VIEW

A key attraction dotted along the shores of Lombardy's lakes are its villas. Sometimes these are palatial residences magnificently adorned with terraces, balustrades, cascades of stairs and statues in great profusion – all enviably endowed with a view of the lake.

Further south, away from the mountain districts, where the hot afternoon sun generates enormous heat in summer, the solution has been to open up the north and south sides of the houses for increased ventilation and to provide no windows at all in the west end where the effects of low sun are almost uncontrollable. This is a great natural alternative to air conditioning.

Vented walls, such as those seen on Umbrian barns, as well as on those in Emilia-Romagna, are widely used in Lombardy and are more common in the hay-raising districts than anywhere else. Although vented walls are generally used in farm storage buildings so that crops may be protected yet sufficiently ventilated, they are also found in other outdoor buildings – chicken coops, pigsties – and occasionally in houses as decoration.

The eastern Po Valley around Mantua (at this point almost into Emilia-Romagna and the Veneto) is particularly rich in examples of decorative air vents. The extraordinary variety of pattern depends on materials (mostly the building materials are brick or terracotta tiles), and on whatever the local traditional patterns might be. In some areas, for example, there might be a Greek cross pattern set in brick. In others bricks might be laid on their sides with alternate rows facing in opposite directions. There is a direct, honest simplicity about these 'decorations' and about the buildings in which they are set.

In contrast to the houses on the plain, Lombardy's lakeside architecture is, mostly, a gentle architecture of houses and villas devoted to pleasure and relaxation rather than simply everyday living. The perfect foil for hectic city life, the lakeside villa, with its combined advantages of fresh air and backdrop of mountains and water, developed from the idea of the *casino di delizie* (roughly translated this means a 'pleasure house', somewhere for use in the summer, say) which became popular in Lombardy in the sixteenth and seventeenth centuries. There are notable examples scattered around Lakes Como, Maggiore and Garda. One in particular, on Maggiore, is the magnificent villa built for the Borromeo family on the little Isola Madre and the gardens and *palazzo* on the adjacent Isola Bella. An airy elegance pervades these buildings where marble is combined with stucco, and outdoor living is just as important as any interior lifestyle.

RIGHT: CANNOBIO
Roughened, textured, battered and weather-beaten, this is the only decoration the stone and brick of this wall is ever likely to receive. Raw pigments the colour of the earth are revealed as the materials gradually flake away and return to dust.

RIGHT: HOMES FOR PEOPLE
AND CATTLE
Hefty flint and stone walls provide protection against the elements in this Lombardian village. At ground level there are barns for housing cattle and for storage, while people live above, under the eaves.

Gardens designed in combination with the architecture were a key attraction on the villas around Lombardy's lakes. Constructed in terraces, they have unexpected turnings, alternately sunny and shady corners, and stairs, vases, balustrades and statues scattered about in great profusion. There is a tendency to over-prettiness in the gardens of the grander villas and affectation in the designs of the villas themselves. Quite different, however, are those built for lesser mortals along the lake shores and on the edges of the towns. As if to compensate for their lack of sculptural adornment, most are brightly painted in colours ranging from terracotta to mustard or pink. Small, often only three storeys high, each floor is separated from the next by a single course of projecting bricks stuccoed over then rendered in colour like the rest of the building.

Those built right at the water's edge, their foundations under water, have a series of undercrofts, half in the water and half out, meant for the storage of boats. Here and there flights of stone-built steps give access from the water to *terra firma*. Here you find fishermen slinging their lines into the water, or people sun-bathing. With their shutters and their wrought-iron balconies hung with washing, these little

RIGHT: MENAGGIO

Built at the edge of Lake Como, the lower building's foundations are in fact underwater. Beyond the pier and slipway, the loggia is still in use and is a cool and restful spot from which to view the lake in the summer heat.

RIGHT: THE OUTSIDE ROOM

Modernized and updated, tightly packed houses at the water's edge utilize whatever space they have available to them, storing boats, fishing tackle, nets and firewood in the undercrofts. Here, cleaned up for twentieth-century living, the cobbled floor points to its original workaday character.

LEFT: PANEL PAINTING
This house at Orta San Giulio flaunts painted panels which match in scale any window or door. Both geometric patterns and pictures of the saints feature as subjects. Wandering down a street like this there is never a dull moment.

LEFT: FAMILY GLORY
Stucco leaves and branches emerging from a plain wall provide support for a stemma, a coat of arms, placed at the summit of a niche. The glory of the household is reflected in this arrangement, which is seen time and time again on Italian houses. Those more concerned with their heritage, or with more to boast about, paint the individual elements of their arms in different colours.

houses, were they not set against great sweeps of mountain and mirrored in often very placid waters, could be on the coast of Liguria.

So could the rough, stone-built villages around the edges of all the lakes. Poised over the water, they are as watchful and as mean as any in Liguria or the Umbrian hills. Most are compact, the narrow streets providing protection against both sun and wind. Houses are often constructed of stone patterned with rust; and, with their rough textured stonework and raw earth colours, they blend in to their surroundings. Nothing could be further in character and outlook from the neighbouring brightly stuccoed lakeside holiday homes.

The Alps, the lakes and the Po are Lombardy's best-known features. The first two are well populated by travellers, the other by farmers. In fact Lombardy is crammed with people. And yet, part of its charm is the impression created by many of the towns and villages in all three parts of isolation and of self-sufficiency.

Rarely do Lombardy's settlements extend outside their old boundaries. In addition, fewer *cascine* are abandoned here than in most other regions; even if the ancient barn is overshadowed by a great modern silo, at least this is a symbol of continuing prosperity.

GLOSSARY

ARCADE: a row of free-standing arches, carried on columns or piers, forming a covered walk.

ARCADING, BLIND: a shallow arcade attached to a wall.

BORGHO (plural *BORGHI*): a little walled village.

CAPITAL: the carved head or top part of a column.

CASA COLONICA: farmhouse.

CASETTE A SCHIERA: a terrace of small workers' houses.

COLONNADE: a row of columns placed at regular intervals, possibly carrying arches.

CORBEL: a block, usually of stone but sometimes of wood, projecting from the face of a wall, supporting a beam or other horizontal member.

FAÇADE: the exterior front or face of a building.

EAVES: the underpart of a sloping roof overhanging a wall.

GRISAILLE: a style of painting on walls or ceilings in greyish tints in imitation of bas-reliefs.

LINTEL: a horizontal beam spanning an opening such as a window or door.

LOGGIA: a gallery open on one or more sides, sometimes arcaded. It can also be a little garden house.

OGEE ARCH: a pointed arch popular throughout the Middle Ages.

PANTILE: a roofing tile whose cross-section forms an S-shaped curve.

PIAZZA: an urban space bounded by buildings – a square.

PILASTER: a rectangular column, or pier, projecting slightly from the wall.

PITCHED ROOF: a roof having two sloping surfaces meeting in a central ridge.

PORTAL: a doorway or gate, particularly one which is rather magnificent.

PORTICO: a roofed space, open or partially enclosed, forming the entrance and centrepiece to a façade.

QUOIN: the dressed stones at the corners of buildings.

STUCCO: plasterwork.

VILLA-FATTORIA: the villa-farmhouse of a landowner.

INDEX OF PLACE NAMES